Praise for You Are

"Through the power of story, *You Are Nc
Generational Trauma and Shame* speaks _____ ,   .
most need to hear these messages. While our rational selves are busy learning
the steps we can follow to unshame ourselves, our more tender parts get to
experience what it feels like to be loved as we are."

—Simona Vivi H, founder of The Center for Remothering and of reMothering.org

"In *You Are Not Your Mother*, author Karen C.L. Anderson unpacks the tricky
territory of shame and how it can color your whole life and hold you back,
unless you face it head on. Childhood can be a minefield of hurt, trauma, and
shame both at school and at home with difficult parents. Anderson's revelatory
courage in sharing her healing journey is inspiring and offers a roadmap to
both mental health and the joy that comes from reclaiming your own life."

—Becca Anderson, author of *Badass Affirmations*

"Both unflinching and compassionate, *You Are Not Your Mother* offers an
unconventional perspective on how shame is passed down through our
maternal lineage and how women and those socialized as women can
manage the often debilitating mind/body experience that is shame."

—Kara Loewentheil, host of the *UnF*ck Your Brain* podcast and author of the
upcoming book *Take Back Your Break*

"This book invites you to be aware. You need that awareness as much as a
conductor needs a score. Without that score, the orchestra will play poorly,
and we will not get music. Without awareness, you will repeat your pratfalls,
retain your pain, never feel quite right, and, history tells us, harm the next
generation. If you are not to be your mother, best open your eyes. This book is
a gentle eye-opener.

—Eric Maisel, bestselling author of *Why Smart People Hurt* and *Redesign
Your Mind*

"Karen C.L. Anderson begins her compassionate book so that we can safely recognize shaming through her—in a timeline of her life experiences in prose poetry, rhythmically punctuating the emotional beats of shock, hurt, freeze, erasure, and breakdown.

"As we further read, think, absorb, and realize the shame within us in stages of understanding, bringing us home to Self, Karen follows our thought processes and centers us in a conceptual framework with the tenderness of an embrace.

"It is in the practices that the brave-hearted work begins, as Karen guides us in many ways to express and objectify our shame through creative, interactive, multisensory activities that move our experiences outward. These lively, improvisational practices delight and challenge since we are free to select, develop, and share their transformative power.

"When we emerge from this deep journey of self-knowing in a reverse timeline with positive, life-affirming reflections of Karen's experiences, we will have made the choice of worthiness, self-acceptance, and self-love, realizing that we are not perfect, but simply human."

—Kate Farrell, author of *Story Power: Secrets to Creating, Crafting, and Telling Memorable Stories*

"In her powerful new book, bestselling author and certified coach Karen C.L. Anderson offers readers an empowering yet practical plan of action to transform shame. Filled with reflective writing topics, mindset reboots, and meditative practices, the book lends hope to anyone struggling in their relationship with a maternal family member. Not only does Anderson share the techniques she has used in her decades of coaching, she pulls back the veil to reveal the difficult and fruitful work she did with her own narcissistic mother to overcome toxic habits, release her shame, and move into open-hearted acceptance. Bonus: it reads like poetry."

—Nita Sweeney, bestselling author of *Depression Hates a Moving Target*

"Karen C.L. Anderson does an amazing job at taking the reader through the raw, vulnerable, and authentic parts of our human nature in *You Are Not Your Mother*. Through her vulnerability, I was able to see myself and not feel alone. The reader gets a clear snapshot of what generational shame looks like, how it's passed down, and what can be done about it. I found so much value in gaining awareness of the messages that are playing in my own head and the guideposts showing me how to create a new relationship with shame. This is a book that I would recommend to any mother or daughter."

—Rachael Wolff, podcaster, speaker and author of *Letters from a Better Me*

"This book has a felt-sense all on its own. From page one, I witnessed the tender waves of my own shame emerge—raw and exposed—but then gently held and nurtured in a new way, as the love infused into each page began to soothe & shift the wounds of a lifetime. Karen's writing is a beautiful blend of incredibly relatable personal experience and integrative body-based healing practices that will guide you to fall in love with the deeply human pieces of yourself, over and over again."

—Samantha Johnson, trauma-centered somatic coach & founder of The Alchemy of Truth

"This is the book every daughter with a difficult mother needs. It is a wise, compassionate guide to liberating yourself from the stories your mother told you about who you are.

"Part poetry, part memoir, part savvy self-help book, Karen combines stories about the deep pain she has experienced in her relationship with her mother with simple tools you can use to help you dismantle and release the emotional grip a lifetime of being shamed creates in your heart and mind.

"If you have had a difficult relationship with your mother, you will recognize the feelings of internalized shame Karen so powerfully illustrates with the stories she shares, and you will know once and for all that you are not alone and that having complicated feelings about your mother is okay.

"Karen is the wise voice you want whispering in your ear when shame knocks on your door, reminding you that you are so much more than your relationship with your mother."

—Maggie Reyes, master certified marriage coach & bestselling author of *The Questions for Couples Journal*

"Powerful. Liberating. Soul food. This book is a journey of transgenerational healing and self-love. Beautifully written, it will awaken parts of your soul that you didn't know were dormant.

"For anyone that has lived with shame, or feels like they lost themselves as a result of being in a dysfunctional relationship, this book will make you feel seen and understood and open doors to freedom and healing. It includes easy-to-follow, powerful exercises that will leave you wondering how you ever coped without them! Karen shows us how to release ourselves from the shackles of shame and step into the beauty and strength of our true selves—unashamedly and with deep self-love.

"Thank you, Karen, for showing me how to love myself again and reignite my inner spark."

—Yasmin Kerkez, co-founder of Family Support Resources

"If you talk mean to yourself, if you let the opinions of others govern your decisions, if you allow cultural expectations and your own history and judgments of others to impact your view of yourself...don't let this book go until you finish it. This book feels like a life-affirming conversation with a trusted friend, the one that you know will tell you the truth, no matter how difficult AND beautiful it is.

"In the first part, I had to remind myself to breathe. The experiences were difficult because I recognized myself in so many of them.

"Through succinct, staccato style, I gather mighty threads that help me attach elements of shame and toss the whole mess in the trash. I can't guess how many times I will give this book to people who are on their way to hack their own path to live without shame.

"And. Let me tell you how delightful it feels to say, 'I am not my mother.' "

—Mary Anne Em Radmacher, author/artist

YOU ARE NOT YOUR MOTHER

Other Books by Karen C.L. Anderson

Difficult Mothers, Adult Daughters: A Guide for Separation, Liberation & Inspiration

The Difficult Mother-Daughter Relationship Journal

Overcoming Creative Anxiety: Prompts & Practices for Disarming Your Inner Critic

YOU ARE NOT YOUR MOTHER

Releasing Generational Trauma and Shame

KAREN C.L. ANDERSON

CORAL GABLES

Cover Design: Elina Diaz
Cover Photo/illustration: stock.adobe.com/Dedraw Studio
Layout & Design: Elina Diaz

For permission requests, please contact the publisher at:
Mango Publishing Group
2850 S Douglas Road, 2nd Floor
Coral Gables, FL 33134 USA
info@mango.bz

For special orders, quantity sales, course adoptions and corporate sales, please email the publisher at sales@mango.bz. For trade and wholesale sales, please contact Ingram Publisher Services at customer.service@ingramcontent.com or +1.800.509.4887.

You Are Not Your Mother: Releasing Generational Trauma and Shame

Library of Congress Cataloging-in-Publication number: 2023934036
ISBN: pb) 978-1-68481-266-0 (hc) 978-1-68481-289-9 (e) 978-1-68481-267-7
BISAC category code: FAM033000, FAMILY & RELATIONSHIPS / Parenting / Parent & Adult Child

This book about shame is full of love.

Table of Contents

FOREWORD

I write the *Rethinking Mental Health* blog for *Psychology Today*, and my usual posts average a few thousand views. I did one called "I Hate My Mother." I looked at the numbers today: that post has had 531,137 views so far. (By contrast, "I Hate My Father" has only had 80,000 views.)

The authoritarian literature, which had its heyday in the 1950s, attempted to answer the following question: "Who were Hitler's followers?" Not, "Who was Hitler?" That was seen as a separate question. No: "Who were his followers, and what did they have in common?"

One of the findings was that as many German women as German men loved and revered Hitler. Tens of millions of German women were devoted to Hitler. Can you imagine what they were like at home?

One of the great secrets, kept secret by exactly those whom you would expect to want to keep it secret, is just how many parents are cruel. Cruel not as in peevish or irritable or short-tempered, but cruel as in terrifyingly, remorselessly cruel.

And their children are not supposed to be affected?

And then that child has children. And *those* children won't be affected?

What stops this intergenerational, multi-generational harm? How can a shamed person not just shame her own children? If your mother was harmed in childhood, and she quite naturally and maybe inevitably harmed you, well, now what? Must you play the hand dealt to you, as if you had no say in the matter, no free will, no chance, and no choice? That's the question, isn't it?

Shame is one of the primary results of tyrannical parents harming their children. The shamed child of one generation becomes the shaming parent of the next generation. Unless she doesn't. We are in an age of talking about and talking out these matters, and, to some extent at least, we are sharing awareness about how not to be cruel parents like our own cruel parents.

Karen C.L. Anderson, by telling her story and by sharing her thoughts, is sharing awareness. She is not saying, "Snap your fingers! This is going to be easy!" She is shedding tears on the page about the experiences she had and shedding more tears about how the consequences of those experiences keep playing themselves out, even though she would wish that they wouldn't, even though she "knows better." She has suggestions, but that isn't precisely the point. The point is more in the territory of radical self-acceptance—which, actually, is a deeply controversial idea.

There is an interesting divide in the Protestant Church as to how one is saved. Some sects believe that you are saved by doing good works. Other sects believe that you are saved by faith alone. There is the same significant divide in the self-help literature. Some writers argue for the necessity of change. Do better. Enter recovery. If you are not the person you want to be, become that person.

Others argue that you are perfectly fine as you are. Love your faults, your flaws, your peculiarities, your pratfalls, your moments of involuntary meanness. Radically and unconditionally accept yourself. If you make the same mistake again—well, that's unfortunate, but still be kind to yourself. Love yourself, have faith in yourself, affirm yourself...period.

Karen invites you to think about this fault line, the one between change and acceptance. Who knows what the answer is? But this book is a beautiful asking of the question. I am perhaps more in the camp of "good works" and Karen is perhaps more in the camp of "faith alone" and perhaps we would never find ourselves in the same congregation. But any given Sunday would find us wrestling with the same question. The question? How to be *now*, given the past? How to be *now*? How to be *now*?

Authoritarian parents are real. They exist. They exist by the millions. They do real harm. They ought not to be excused because (or if) they have been harmed themselves. But that is its own separate question. The reader of this book will be someone who has been deeply, negatively affected by her mother. She can choose to love her mother or hate her mother, keep in touch with her mother or keep her distance from her mother, but all of those are separate questions. The main question is: Can she bring the sort of self-awareness to her situation that allows her to see what has happened, what she intends to do, and how she intends to be?

This book invites you to be aware. You need that awareness as much as a conductor needs a score. Without that score, the orchestra will play poorly, and we will not get music. Without awareness, you will repeat your pratfalls, retain your pain, never feel quite right, and, history tells us, harm the next generation. If you are not to be your mother, best open your eyes. This book is a gentle eye-opener.

Eric Maisel, PhD

PREFACE

2021

I am lying on the bathroom floor.

Even though I just threw up, I am not sick.

This isn't a stomach bug.

It's not food poisoning.

It's a purge. A release. A letting go.

A vision comes to me as I lie there.

Women standing next to each other, stretching into infinity.

One woman hands a box to another woman, who takes it with one hand and, without examining its contents, tucks it inside her heart, while simultaneously using her other hand to take it out and hand it to yet another woman, who does the same with someone else, and so on.

Each time the box changes hands, it looks a little different, but inside... inside are the same messages: I'm not okay. I'm unworthy. There is something wrong with me. I am bad.

I whisper to them: "It's not yours."

"Fareeda knew her granddaughter could never understand how shame could grow and morph and swallow someone until she had no choice but to pass it along so that she wasn't forced to bear it alone.... She saw the chain of shame passed from one woman to the next so clearly now, saw her place in the cycle so vividly.... She was seized to confess, at last, the fear that circled her brain in endless loops: that she would do the same thing to her daughters that Mama had done to her. That she would force them to repeat her life."

—Etaf Rum, in her *New York Times* bestselling novel, *A Woman Is No Man* (with gracious thanks to Etaf Rum for her permission to use this quote)

PART I

A TIMELINE OF TRAUMA, DISCONNECTION, AND SHAME

"...shame is like laughter. And inspiration. It doesn't knock."

—Stephen King, in his novel *Fairy Tale*

They say that children can't remember much before the age of four, unless the memories are repeatedly retold and strengthened over time.

They also say that human memory is faulty, no matter how old you are.

Not to mention that if you experienced any sort of trauma in the first few years of your life, you may not consciously remember what happened, but your body does.

Your body remembers.

0–5

They Fight

I wake up.

They are screaming and hitting.

I am crying.

I am two.

My Hair Is Sticky

I am sitting in my highchair.

I won't eat my cereal.

My mother dumps the bowl over my head.

I freeze.

And then I cry.

My hair is sticky.

The Kitten Dies

I am playing with my dolls in a closet in the apartment above the real estate office and beauty parlor.

I am alone.

———

I go to kindergarten when I am four because my mother needs to work.

One time, I have to stand in the corner because I was talking too much.

I go to the Kanzows' after kindergarten so they can take care of me.

I find a big white rock outside and carry it to the door to show Mrs. Kanzow.

The rock slips out of my fingers and lands on a kitten at my feet.

It's dead.

I hide in a room between a bed and the wall.

She Throws Up in the Parking Lot

My mother picks me up from kindergarten in the turquoise Volkswagen Beetle. She opens the driver's side door and throws up.

I disappear.

———

They are sick and throwing up.

I climb onto the kitchen counter and get myself some cereal.

There's a Wedding

Even though I get to be the Flower Girl, I cry so hard my new stepfather has to pick me up and carry me out of the church.

Later, I dance at the reception wearing my yellow dress, white tights, and shiny black patent leather Mary Janes.

There's a photo that proves it.

5–10

What I Did

I'm standing at the blackboard in my second-grade classroom after school, writing my numbers from one to a hundred.

It's my punishment for calling one of my classmates a crybaby.

My face feels hot and prickly.

There's a pit in my stomach.

I can't breathe.

I want to disappear.

I felt the same way a few days before when my mother made me tell my stepfather, in graphic detail, about what I had done with some neighborhood kids in the woods.

It was a "you show me yours and I'll show you mine" situation that went beyond showing to touching.

I can barely get the words out because I am crying so hard.

I wanted to disappear then, too.

That's why I was, a few days later, trying to offload that experience onto my classmate.

I get home from school and stand in front of a mirror.

I make my eyes get hard and squinty.

"I hate you. You're so ugly."

I scratch at my face.

I am bad.

They Take Pictures of Me

My mother and stepfather take me somewhere and we spend the night in a hotel.

All I have is my winter nightgown. It is hot so they give me one of my stepfather's T-shirts to sleep in.

My mother wants to take a picture of me in the T-shirt. I don't want her to.

I hide in the bathroom but I can't hold the door against them.

I run to the bed and hide under the bedcovers but I'm not strong enough. They tear them off.

As I run around the room trying to hide, they take pictures of me.

They think it's funny.

What I want doesn't matter.

I am powerless.

I Can't Swallow the Lima Beans

I'm sitting alone at the dining room table.

My mother is in the kitchen and my stepfather is standing in the doorway watching me.

On my plate is a pile of cold lima beans congealed with margarine.

I ruin dinner because I refuse to eat them. They coax and threaten and laugh and roll their eyes and tell me there are starving children in Africa who would be grateful to have my lima beans.

I want to disappear.

They lose their patience.

Frustrated, my mother gets up to do the dishes.

"You will sit there until you eat them," my stepfather says. "And if you don't eat them now, you'll have them for breakfast."

Tears run down my face.

I take a forkful, put it in my mouth, chew a couple of times, try to swallow, and gag it back up onto my plate.

"*That* will be your breakfast tomorrow!" my stepfather says through clenched teeth.

I am a selfish, spoiled brat.

She's Disgusted

"The doctor says she's chunky," my mother says to my stepfather, after a visit to the pediatrician.

I perceive her disgust, fear, frustration, and...amusement?

I disappear.

Something is wrong with me.

He Drives Drunk

I am in the passenger seat.

My stepfather is driving me home from choir practice.

He's drunk.

He slams on the brakes and swears.

"But they had their blinker on!" I say.

He mutters under his breath.

He pulls into the garage and slowly turns to look at me with a blank face.

I disappear.

I Have a Selfish Nature

We are visiting my great grandparents in New Hampshire. They are meeting Billy, my adopted brother, for the first time.

My great-grandmother asks us to present our palms to her for her to read.

Billy offers his hand with his fingers spread open.

I offer mine with my fingers closed together.

She takes our hands in hers and says, "This shows that Billy has a generous nature and Karen has a selfish nature."

See?

10–15

Too Many Fritos

"It's not my fault," I hear my mother say to my grandmother, who is berating her over the phone for me being fat.

I disappear.

———

I am sick in the middle of the night from eating too many Fritos.

I don't make it to the bathroom.

My mother is disgusted and angry.

Extra-Large?

We are clothes shopping at Jaymars.

I am in the dressing room.

My mother tugs and pulls at the top I've put on.

It's too small.

"I don't know if they have an extra-large," she says, exasperated and embarrassed.

When she asks Mrs. Krafick, who works there, if they have an extra-large, she has that look on her face:

sort of smiling, but also sort of cringing.

I Must Not Want It

I'm scrambling to finish the extra chores I was given so I could raise the money to go on the sixth-grade trip to Washington, DC. It's the last day to make the payment, and I haven't earned enough.

As the minutes and hours tick forward, I am desperate. I beg for more chores.

"Go get my slippers and I'll pay you ten cents," my stepfather offers.

And still it isn't enough.

I am sure I'm not going to Washington, DC, because I haven't earned it. I haven't worked hard enough. I must not want it enough.

I want to disappear.

At the last minute, they sigh and say, "Okay, fine; we'll chip in the last dollar."

I am a pathetic loser.

I Eat Them All

I'm taking care of the neighbor's cats. Judy & Charlie live across the street.

They're cool. They don't have kids. They travel a lot.

When I take care of the cats, I can be alone in their quiet house.

I find Ayds "candies" in the kitchen cupboard.

They aren't candy, they are an appetite suppressant disguised as candy.

I eat them all.

The next time I take care of the cats, there are more Ayds.

I eat them all.

15–20

Forty-Nine Dollars Short

I am standing at the cash register at my after-school job as a cashier at AG Market.

I've been taught how to count back change to the customers, but as the line gets longer and longer, I get nervous and start to disappear.

I am confused.

The next day, I find out from the boss that my register was forty-nine dollars short, meaning I'd given customers more change than they were actually due.

He fires me.

My mother is embarrassed.

He Drops His Pants

My first college mixer.

There's dancing and drinking.

I meet a boy from the football team.

He dances with me.

He holds my hand.

He asks me to take a walk with him.

He drops his pants and tells me to give him a blowjob.

I disappear.

He quickly becomes disgusted with me, either because I have no idea what I am doing or because I won't do it.

I don't know because I disappeared.

He walks away and never speaks to me again.

I Must Be So Unhappy

I am sitting on the floor of the "phone booth" in my dorm listening to my mother tell me, after a visit home, that she can tell I have gained weight.

"You must be so unhappy," she says.

I disappear.

I Get Fired...Again

I am visiting my father and stepmother for the summer in between my sophomore and junior year of college.

I get a job cleaning hotel rooms. I hate it. I get fired.

I cry because I will have to go back home.

My stepmother is furious because I am crying in front of my little sister and brother.

She hisses at me: "How dare you upset them like this."

I am bad.

I Have Sex for the First Time AND Get Pregnant AND He's Gay

It's my senior year.

I meet Michael, a freshman. He says he's bi.

He is a tall and slender and wears eyeliner and has hair dyed strawberry blonde. He wears Aramis cologne.

We go to clubs, drink, and dance to Wham!, Culture Club, and Duran Duran.

I wear a leather miniskirt, fishnet stockings, an off-the-shoulder top, and a long string of fake pearls.

I take half a tab of LSD.

The pearls break and start bouncing on the dance floor in animated slow-motion plumes of light.

Michael and I sleep together without "sleeping together."

Until we do.

———

I go to bed early.

My face is to the wall.

I feel Michael climb into bed and spoon me.

He slides his hands along my body and tells me how good I feel.

I hear laughter. It's not Michael in bed with me, it's my roommate's boyfriend, and there's a crowd of people, including Michael, laughing at me.

I disappear.

Michael and I have sex.

I wake up the next morning and know I am pregnant.

My mother insists I have an abortion.

Not that I have plans to the contrary.

Less than a month later, I have that abortion.

(Of all the things I have experienced shame around, having an abortion is not one of them.)

Michael breaks up with me.

I am devastated.

My mother rolls her eyes. "Can't you see he's gay??!"

21+

Nothing. Nothing. Nothing.

I am living with my mother in her condo after graduating from college.

I am commuting to New York City for my first job.

I have a boyfriend and am madly in love.

One evening he comes over to hang out with me.

She comes home. She is drunk. Her face is blank.

I start to disappear.

He says, "Hi, Ms. _____."

"Go f*ck yourself, _____," she replies.

I disappear.

I "come to" and frantically call him, my fingers shaking as I punch at the buttons on the phone on the wall in the kitchen.

He isn't home yet so I ask his mother to have him call me back.

I stand there waiting for him to call me back. Nothing.
Nothing. Nothing.

But my body knows.

I race upstairs to my mother's room and she's sitting there in her bra and slip, a smirk on her face, with the upstairs phone off the hook.

"F*ck you!" I say through clenched teeth.

"F*CK YOU!" I scream.

I grab my purse and keys and leave.

I don't come back.

Because I Am Fat

He breaks up with me the day before New Year's Eve.

I am devastated.

I am sure it's because I am fat.

Grandma Bribes Me

My grandmother sends me an article about dieting and weight loss.

She says she'll pay me to lose weight.

I disappear.

He Punches Me in the Face

The guy I am "dating" (no, we aren't dating, we are meeting up to have sex, but I can't say that) wants me to give him a blowjob.

I try.

I gag.

He pushes my head down.

My teeth get in the way.

He punches me in the face.

I disappear.

Maybe?

My father visits.

I lament that I don't have a boyfriend.

My father says, quietly and with what seems like care, "Maybe if you lost some weight...?"

I disappear.

I Am So Frightened I Can't Speak

I travel to Missouri with my stepfather and his new wife.

We are visiting his parents and extended family there.

We drive to Branson for a concert. There's a lot of stop-and-go traffic.

All of a sudden, he stops the car in the middle of the road, gets out, and unzips his pants.

But it's too late. He wet his pants. He is drunk.

His new wife slides into the driver's seat and swears because it's all wet with urine.

He turns and looks at me in the back seat.

His face is blank.

When we arrive, I am so frightened I can't talk.

I'm twenty-five years old, for crying out loud. What's wrong with me?

I disappear.

I Won't Go to a Hotel to Have Sex,
But I Will Do It in the Backseat of His Car

I walk into Teddy's nightclub at the Holiday Inn in Danbury, Connecticut, with my mother, and meet a guy.

He's tall, dark, and handsome. From Brazil.

We talk. We dance. He probably buys me a drink. We might kiss. Maybe.

He asks me to meet him there again. The next night? Maybe. Whatever. We make a date to meet there again.

I show up at the appointed time. He doesn't. I wait. In the lobby. Because it's a date. With him. I'm not "available" anymore. I'm not there to meet someone else.

So I wait.

Every time the door opens, I turn, expectantly.

Finally. There he is. An hour late?

He's with some other guys...friends of his. He seems almost surprised to see me.

He walks into the bar with his friends and I trail along behind them.

We talk. We dance. He probably buys me a drink. We might kiss. Maybe.

He says: "Let's go to a hotel."

I start to disappear, but not before I say no.

Instead, we drive to a deserted parking lot and have sex in the back seat of his car.

A cop shows up and knocks on the window.

I marry him because he needs a green card.

He cheats on me. He hurts me with words. He is disgusted by me. He pretends he's going to stick me with a needle.

He takes pilot lessons.

I wish for him to crash and die because I'd rather be a "grieving widow" than to have to do what I know I have to do.

I file for divorce.

Why can't I make him love me?

I never met his family. Or even spoke to them. I don't think they know I exist.

Because I have disappeared.

I Have Love to Give

I meet another guy at Teddy's.

He says he can tell that I have a lot of love to give.

He is also tall, dark, and handsome, but so different from the guy I married. For one, he's from India, not Brazil.

He's also kind. He's also polite.

He introduces me to his mother, who is visiting from India. "This is my friend Karen," he says.

Every December, he leaves the country and travels for a month and a half.

I spend one New Year's Eve alone.

I spend the next one with my ex.

When he comes back, he lavishes me with gifts from his travels.

He tells me he's going to be out of state on the weekends, doing work on is PhD at a well-known university.

A friend says she sees him at a local bar with another woman.

Some version of this happens about once a month.

I confront him, crying. Wanting for him to be the one I give my love to.

How can someone who doesn't really exist give anything?

A Turning Point

I place a personal ad on AOL's Romance Connection looking for a New Year's Eve date because there's a part of me—a very small part—that knows I can do better than men who are cruel to me and treat me as an afterthought.

As a result, I meet the man who will become my husband three years later.

This relationship is a turning point.

He has no idea. LOL.

But really, neither do I.

A note from current me: It is around this time that I start to experience anxiety, specifically a phobia of throwing up and of other people throwing up.

Activities that were once fun and exciting (like flying) become terrifying.

I am not afraid of the plane crashing, I am afraid that someone on the plane will throw up. Turbulence is scary because someone might get airsick.

Just reading about a rise in stomach flu in the newspaper makes my heart pound and my knees go weak.

As the years go by, I wonder if I will be unable to leave my house. My father had a similar experience with anxiety. He refused to fly and limited himself from a variety of activities due to his phobias and anxiety.

That doesn't happen because I force myself to continue to fly and experience significant anxiety and panic attacks when I do. I don't realize how overriding my nervous system like this doesn't help.

Then I become unable to be the passenger in a car when someone else is driving. This impacts the relationship I have with my husband, whom I logically know is one of the safest and most skilled drivers I know. My startle reflex becomes magnified. I flinch at everything and cling to the handle that hangs from the car ceiling. I make him slow down. In certain situations, like heavy rain, I make him pull over.

My anxiety and the way it manifests become one more thing that triggers debilitating shame.

Until I understand two things:

1. *I have complex PTSD and am experiencing emotional flashbacks.*
2. *I am not telling the truth about myself to myself or to others.*

He Pulls a Garbage Can Over

He's spending the weekend with me. When he arrives, he says he has a headache and doesn't feel well.

He says he's going to lie down for a while. He pulls a garbage can next to the bed.

I feel a dropping sensation in my body.

I disappear.

Literally.

I leave and drive away.

Hours later, I come back and peek in the windows to see if he's okay.

Not Her Fault(?)

I tell my mother that I might be addicted to carbs.

"What a relief," she says. "I'm just glad it's not my fault."

A Double Wedding?

We call my mother to tell her we are engaged.

She tells me that she has also met a guy. They come for a visit. She suggests that maybe we can have a double wedding.

I decline.

She asks me if, at my wedding, I will give her my bouquet instead of doing the traditional bouquet toss.

Forty Pounds

I go on fen-phen to lose weight.

I lose about forty pounds.

I marry the guy.

Even When I Test Him

I start having recurring dreams about my husband cheating on me.

The worst part isn't that he's cheating, it's why.

"Of course I'm cheating on you...you're pathetic," the husband-in-my-dream says, his voice dripping with contempt.

Meanwhile the husband-in-real-life loves me unconditionally.

Even when I test him. Like by regaining the forty pounds and then some. Like when I try to tell him how to parent his kids (the way I was parented).

I cannot imagine him saying to me that I am pathetic.

I don't know unconditional love until I meet him.

> *Note from current me: There are still times I don't think I deserve his unconditional love...that's part of what qualifies me to write this book.*

Rage

My fourteen-year-old stepdaughter lies to me about something.

I tell my husband, her father, that I will handle it.

I call her and ask about it. She denies it, even though I have proof.

Then she tells me she and her two brothers are taking their father out for Father's Day and hangs up. Off they go.

Rage rises up in me like a volcano spewing deep, hot, intense anger.

And then tears. I cry long and hard and inconsolably.

This is the rage-devastation-shame cycle.

What previous me didn't know that current me knows is that I was triggered. I was experiencing intense emotional distress in the face of something that reminded my body, but not my conscious self, of past events that were traumatic to me. My body didn't know how to distinguish between an actual threat to my life and normal teen girl behavior. If teenaged me had been caught lying, she wouldn't have been so flip about it...she'd have been curled up in a shame spiral, just like she was that day her stepdaughter lied to her. And she certainly wouldn't have taken her father out for lunch.

Total Loser

We are visiting my mother and her new husband.

I get the idea to ask her: "If you had to go back and be with one of your former husbands, who would you choose, my father or my stepfather?"

Without hesitation, she replies: "Your stepfather, of course, because your father was a total loser."

My stepfather, the alcoholic who beat her. Who abused me.

She'd choose him over my father.

Rage surges in my body but it's not safe here.

I disappear.

When it is safe, on the hour-plus car ride home, I cry so hard my shirt is soaked. I sob to exhaustion.

They Don't Want Me

The magazine I've been the editor of since 1997 is sold to another company and the new company doesn't want me.

My nearly twenty years as a plastics industry trade magazine editor are unceremoniously over.

"I Know Better"

My younger sister (same father, different mother) is getting married.

I've met her husband-to-be and I have opinions.

I project my insecurities and shame onto her/them.

I think I "know better."

I say things on family calls that are cruel.

She is hurt.

We stop talking to each other.

I Can't Repeat Those Words

I am sitting in the living room of a hypnotherapist and Emotional Freedom Techniques (EFT) practitioner.

She asks me to repeat after her (while tapping): "Even though I am overweight, I love and accept myself."

I can't repeat after her because I am crying so hard I can't speak.

I can't say those words.

College Dream, 1.0

I am having recurring dreams about graduating from college.

In the dream, I can't find my dorm room, I can't find my classrooms, I get way behind on homework, I don't show up for final exams, and so on.

And then I am at graduation about to get my diploma, and I know the truth and "they" probably do too: I probably don't have enough credits.

Rather than finding out ahead of time, I wait to be found out.

———

In my waking life, I write to get my transcripts.

My final GPA is 2.9.

My face burns. I crumple inside.

She Gives Me the Finger

We are visiting my mother.

It's summer and she is in the kitchen and I am outside on the deck.

I see her looking out the window.

I walk to the window and smile at her.

She looks at me with a sneer on her face, lifts her hand, and raises her middle finger.

I disappear.

I don't remember what happens next.

Later I am both furious and devastated.

I tell anyone who will listen what she did.

The responses range from shock ("What kind of mother does that??!")

...to practical ("That's about her, not you.")

...to quizzical ("Why are you taking it so personally? I would have laughed if my mother did that.").

I shame myself for years when I think about that moment (and others like it) because I took it so personally. That in my mind makes me pathetic. I mean, I'd read The Four Agreements, one of which is "Don't take anything personally."

So why do I take it so personally?

Secretly Relieved

I regain weight that had been lost.

My knees hurt.

I am diagnosed with Lyme disease.

I am secretly relieved. Maybe I can blame the Lyme disease for my weight gain.

I start blogging to see if I can "love and accept myself" enough to lose the weight again.

Delete. Delete. Delete.

My mother sends me an email and tells me she's disappointed in the person I've become.

Among other things.

Cue the fury, devastation, and shame.

I start to write back, defending myself.

Delete. Delete. Delete.

"I am done. Do not call or email me again," I write.

I cut her out of my life.

And I cut myself in.

My Heart Pounds

My grandmother asks me to become her legal guardian, health care conservator, and power of attorney.

I accept.

I am now legally required to be in contact with my mother, but only to send her monthly updates about her mother.

When I see an email from my mother in my inbox, my heart pounds and my breathing becomes shallow.

I want to disappear.

And then I roll my eyes at myself and think I am pathetic.

She Thinks I Am Stupid

My mother sends me an email asking about my grandmother's finances.

Just seeing it in my inbox makes my heart pound. My breathing becomes shallow. I feel a dropping sensation in my core.

Then I read it.

The dropping sensation becomes lava erupting out of me.

White. HOT! RAGE!!

She thinks I'm stupid.

And I am afraid she's right.

I have created an identity for myself.

A shame-based identity.

Of course I have. How could I not have?

I am her victim. A bad, selfish, spoiled brat, a pathetic victim.

Because I believe her.

I Show Up as Needing to Be Fixed

I attend a retreat.

In the months leading up to it, I am conflicted.

Part of me wants to go and another part definitely does not.

My experience with these types of events is that I go, intending it to be fun and empowering, and then somewhere along the line, I find myself feeling insecure, small, and powerless.

It happens so fast that I am blindsided by it.

Shame doesn't knock.

Then the next time I think, "Oh, I've got this now…it won't happen again."

And then it happens again in a slightly different way, but it's all based on the same story:

In an effort to impress and/or get the approval of the female authority figure, I will "forget" what I really want and start wanting what I think she thinks I should want.

I will show up as needing to be fixed. And I won't be able to control it.

I am so disconnected from myself.

Pathetic.

I try to get her attention and praise. I call out answers or raise my hand immediately. I try to interact with her in between sessions or at meals.

Later I experience that familiar sensation.

I want to be seen as smart and quick and valuable by her, to be recognized. Yet even when I am seen and recognized, I feel terrible afterwards.

I want to disappear.

The voice inside me says:

Who do you think you are? Stop it. Stop calling attention to yourself. You're being selfish. You're not clever. They don't want to hear what you have to say. Stop trying. It's ugly. You're not a child, for crying out loud.

Despite my best efforts, despite being aware of this, it still happens. Like a beach ball being held under water, it woooooshes back up to the surface. The deeper I try and hold it down, the higher it shoots above the surface once released.

So when I am invited by a beloved mentor to help her teach and train at a week-long certification event, I am thrilled. Honored.

And full of dread.

My bowels won't let me sleep. I think it's because I'm nervous about flying.

What I don't see is that I am holding the truth of myself under the water because I don't want "pathetic loser" to show up and embarrass me in front of my mentor and the others at this event.

It's as if I sleepwalk through the week.

I know I am there.

I know I am participating.

And yet, I have disappeared.

"What's Wrong with Karen?"

I meet a group of women at a writing retreat and we decide that we're going to do this on our own every year.

It's wonderful and amazing until it isn't.

I force myself to want to be part of it, because I think it's what I should want.

After hearing mother and grandmother disparage other women my whole life, I can't be like them.

These women want to meet in person not just once a year but twice.

They want to meet every month via Zoom.

And I continue to force myself to do it even though I don't really want to. It's not that they're not wonderful women, it's that I don't want to do the part where we critique each other's writing.

But I haven't let myself not want to.

I travel to Los Angeles for a retreat and my anxiety is at a fever pitch. I am eating Xanax like it's candy.

I have a complete and total meltdown.

I can't control it or myself.

Later, I can hear them whispering about me. "What's wrong with Karen?"

And yet I continue to force myself.

Until I finally stop.

I let myself quit.

Add Entitled to the List

We live in a brand-new house in a brand-new development.

As other houses are built and I see the features and other options that are being incorporated into the designs, I feel envious and regretful that I hadn't thought about or asked for such features and options.

I'm a pathetic loser because I didn't think ahead *and* I am a selfish, spoiled (entitled, privileged) brat because I am not happy with a brand-new house.

I Lie to My Stepdaughter

We travel to Georgia, where my stepdaughter and her family are living because her husband, a naval submariner, is stationed there.

Her husband is on deployment, and she is in need of a well-deserved break.

We are going to watch the grandkids overnight so she and a friend can go to a concert.

We have a hotel, but on the night she's away, we will, of course, stay at their house.

Except at the last minute I decide I can't do it.

I won't be able to sleep.

I am terrified one of the children will throw up.

I stay in the hotel and my husband stays with his grandchildren.

The next day, I lie to my stepdaughter when she calls and asks how it went.

I say it went fine.

I am bad.

The Puppy Has Diarrhea in Her Crate

For the first time in my adult life, and in our marriage, we have a dog.

A puppy.

My husband has wanted a dog for as long as I've known him.

I brought two cats to the marriage, and we've had cats ever since.

The puppy has digestive issues.

My husband, the nurturing one, the one who we agreed would do the poop and puke duty, has outpatient surgery and is told to take it easy because any complication could be serious.

That night the puppy has diarrhea in her crate, not once, not twice, but three times.

I am angry. Not at the puppy.

My husband gets up to help clean the crate after the second round of diarrhea.

I am struck by rage.

Between clenched teeth I tell him to get back in bed because I don't want to have to take care of both of them if he causes himself a complication.

The next morning, exhausted, I take the pup for a walk and, when we get back, she won't come inside.

I coax and tug a bit on the leash.

She resists.

The rage comes back. I picture myself yanking her into the house.

Instead, I gently pick her up, carry her in, and then hide in a closet, where I sob with shame.

I want to send the dog back because I don't think I can do this.

I am bad.

I am a selfish, spoiled brat.

PART II

THE CONTEXT

CHAPTER 1

WHAT EXACTLY IS SHAME?

Those are moments of emotional trauma and shame from my life.

They are moments when I took messages that were not mine and internalized them—made them part of my nature and identity and lived with that internalized shame running the show. I didn't do this consciously or "on purpose." It happened automatically because that's what human nervous systems do, especially very young nervous systems.

> **"When a child is not supported or doesn't feel safe navigating various human experiences like shock, panic, shame, anger or fear, the nervous system will not have the conditions to regulate these emotions, so it will shut down, avoid, or disconnect."**
> —Ally Wise, a.k.a. Awaken with Ally, on Instagram

What exactly is shame?

Shame is a painful, destructive, and nearly unbearable experience— one made up of thoughts, feelings, sensations, movements, postures, and internal voices and images—that creates both a disconnection from yourself and a barrier between yourself and others.

It comes from being made to believe (and then internalizing the belief) that there is something fundamentally wrong with you. This can come in the form of harsh criticism or judgment from a caregiver or other person who is important to you. It can also come from abuse.

"What's wrong with you?!"

And

"You should be ashamed of yourself!"

quickly become...

"What's wrong with me?!"

"I'm bad."

"There's something wrong with me."

"I'm not okay the way I am."

The older you become, the more "sophisticated" these thoughts become. They come to feel more "factual"...like you're reporting the weather.

"I'm being ridiculous."

It sounds so innocuous, maybe even humorous. But what "ridiculous" means is deserving or inviting derision or mockery; absurd.

These sentences-in-your-brain are not facts at all. You simply live like they are.

———

My shame experiences are inextricably tied to events that were traumatic to me and that are not uncommon: my parents' divorce and the subsequent perceived abandonment by my father when I was two (although we maintained an "every six weeks" relationship); emotional neglect; and verbal, emotional, and physical violence.

It wasn't these experiences alone that created the shame: it was also generated by my being taught that my body's responses to these traumas were a sign of weakness. My neediness seemingly disgusted my mother, and her disgust created shame in me.

As a child, I could not distinguish between a judgment about my behavior, my body, or my emotions from a judgment about who I am as a person. This left me unable to fully trust myself, my emotions, and my experiences.

These weren't things done to me on purpose by bad people. They were done by people who, because of their own trauma and shame, were often unsafe people.

I didn't experience my mother's intentions, I experienced her unhealed trauma and shame. I experienced her fear. I experienced her as being "unsafe" because that's how she was experiencing herself.

> **"Love, as an intention, when not embodied, becomes fear, and this is what the child experiences."**
> **—Ally Wise**

But shame isn't just that. It is not an experience that comes only from early childhood trauma or from being abused or harshly judged and criticized.

It also comes when those who witness you being abused or harshly criticized, or those whom you tell about the abuse and criticism, meet you with denial, disgust, dismissal, or suggestions that you deserve it.

This is what therapist David Bedrick, founder of the Santa Fe Institute of Shame-Based Studies, calls a shaming witness.

"If this happens early or repetitively, we internalize that witness. When later criticisms and abuse happen, we don't respond from our natural reaction to being hurt. Instead, we don't trust ourselves, don't believe ourselves, and think that something is wrong with us. We don't have a loving, self-protective, self-trusting layer around us that helps us process and respond. That is shame."

—David Bedrick

And because shame is so painful, it can, in and of itself, also be traumatic.

"Shame is a combination of an emotion and a freeze state."

—Dr. Bret Lyon

The moments from my life I described were perceived by my nervous system as threats. And with all its wisdom and intelligence, my body did exactly as it was designed to do. In those moments, I disappeared and disconnected. It's the Freeze in the Flight/Fight/Freeze/Fawn sequence that happens when a threat is perceived.

As a child (and sometimes even now as an adult), I found it hard to use my words, or I was afraid to use my words. I couldn't fight because I was too little. I couldn't run away for the same reason.

My body learned a pattern: freeze, appease, please, and perform. If anger is present, shut it down immediately.

That led to something else that helped shame take root: Those around me "pathologized" the way I—and my body—responded, and were often trying to figure out what was "wrong" with me, rather than seeing what had happened to me as wrong.

The other thing that shame and emotional trauma did was to make it nearly impossible for me to see and know myself clearly. For decades, every encounter, every relationship, every situation, every conversation was filtered through a lens of shame.

It was like a pair of glasses I put on and don't know I am able to take off.

Once I started to understand the dynamic, I became obsessed with shame and overcoming it.

Brené Brown urged me to confront my shame head-on.

I spent years trying to rid myself of shame. I believed that if I tried hard enough, I would no longer think the words, "I'm bad, I'm a selfish spoiled brat, I'm a pathetic loser."

I would no longer experience the crushing, soul-sucking, face prickling, collapsing sensation that I know to be shame.

I would no longer let shame be the driver of my life. I would no longer do "stupid" things. I would feel confident and certain, and my life (and body) would reflect it.

Because as long as I experienced it, I believed that I must deserve to experience it.

Until.

Until I was able to take off those glasses and become a compassionate witness to myself.

When I took off the glasses, it was miraculous. I was able to see myself without that lens of "I'm not okay...there's something wrong with me" clouding my vision.

I stopped hustling for my worthiness. Brené would be so proud of me.

And then boom...I'd put the glasses back on.

Not because I'm stupid. Not because I'm masochistic. And certainly not because there's actually something wrong with me.

But because at first it didn't feel safe to see myself and the world without them. There were people who didn't like it when I took off the glasses. They were confused and/or felt threatened and/or betrayed.

Logically I knew it was safe to take them off and I was able to spend time with them off. But not in all situations and not with all people.

Now, I know how to guide myself through the times when I inevitably put the glasses back on, and I am able to spend more and more time with them off.

> **"Shame comes from an abuse or trauma not lovingly witnessed. Shame happens when the outer witnessing does not mirror and validate our actual experience and we begin to think, 'Something is wrong with me.'"**
> —David Bedrick

That is what happened to me, and it may be what happened to you. Then we internalized it and were unable to meet ourselves with compassion. So we became our own abusers.

> **"In other words, the shaming that occurred with regard to the earlier abuse is perpetuated and perseverates without our even knowing it."**
> —David Bedrick

Until we do know it.

CHAPTER 2

HOW DO YOU GET THERE FROM HERE?

This book is not a clinical or scholarly exploration of generational trauma and shame. Nor does it address healing or repairing such trauma and shame in a clinical or scholarly fashion. For those types of references, please see the Resources section at the end of the book.

What this book does provide is a down-to-earth, conversational, loving, and human approach to understanding it and relating to it differently.

Trauma and shame are not the same thing, but they are often closely associated and don't start with us.

Here's how it goes down.

1. **Shame is handed to you (unconsciously and unintentionally).**

   You might have been socialized by your mother to believe that there's something wrong with you, not because your mother is a bad person, but because she was socialized the same way. Shaming and other forms of oppression are seen as "protective"—a way to remain safe and connected to resources in a culture/system that:

   - doesn't value women equally
   - punishes women when they don't conform to the norms of the culture and/or system

2. **You take it and internalize it and it becomes part of your identity (unconsciously and unintentionally).**

In order to fit in and survive, you go along with it. This isn't a conscious decision you're making. It's happening on a nervous system level.

3. **You live your life with internalized shame running the show (unconsciously and unintentionally).**

The first part of this book provides many examples of what it looks like to live a life with shame running the show. You will have the opportunity to explore your own stories in the Practices section.

4. **You become aware that what you are experiencing is shame (consciously).**

Something happens. There's a turning point—a disturbance in the force. You blink your eyes a few times as if waking up. You make the connection.

5. **You begin to identify your shame-based beliefs and to know when you're experiencing shame (consciously and intentionally).**

You know what shame feels like in your body. You're able to see and hear the sentences in your head. You're able to trace these beliefs back to specific moments in your life.

6. **You start to recognize that experiencing shame does not mean you are bad, wrong, pathetic, not enough, too much, etc. (consciously and intentionally).**

In these moments, you see that experiencing shame doesn't mean anything. You observe it rather than being it. You start to see yourself separate from it.

7. **You create an unshamed identity (consciously and intentionally).**

   Using moments from your life that you loved experiencing, you begin to create resources that you can rely on over and over again to remind you of who you really are and want to be. These resources can't be taken away from you. Yes, your brain still offers shame-based beliefs, but they are no longer facts. You no longer identify with them. This is because you are practicing thinking what your unshamed self believes.

8. **You're able to take care of yourself when you do experience shame (consciously and intentionally).**

   It's unlikely that you will stop experiencing shame 100 percent. But you are able to catch yourself sooner when you do, and when you catch yourself, you're able to tap back into your unshamed identity. Instead of beating yourself up for not having conquered shame for once and for all, you remind yourself, "How human of me. *Of course* I am experiencing shame."

9. **Your relationship to shame changes, and it no longer carries the charge it once did (consciously and intentionally).**

   Unshaming becomes your practice. You're able to talk about your shame-based beliefs and maybe even laugh about them. You might notice yourself feeling the urge to go down the shame spiral but you don't.

CHAPTER 3

HOW AND WHY DOES SHAME GET PASSED DOWN FROM OUR MOTHERS?

Speaking of pathologizing, I kind of hate how pathologizing this is going to sound, but it's because of:

- the patriarchal conditioning women and those socialized as female receive, going back thousands of years, combined with generational trauma and internalized shame

- a lack of understanding of trauma and what it does to our holistic selves, not to mention that acknowledging trauma or seeking help was (and is still) seen as weak and shameful

- racism, white supremacy, misogyny, poverty, and so many other intersections and aspects of a culture that doesn't value women equally

Also, some mothers—especially those in the Baby Boomer and Silent Generations—were taught to be disconnected from themselves and their emotions and to believe that there was something inherently wrong with them. They were thus ill-equipped and un-resourced for motherhood the way it had been configured and laid out for them:

You shall marry a man; he will work; you will have his babies and raise them by yourself in your own home without help; you will ignore your instincts and intuition and outsource your wisdom to "experts" without question; you will raise these children to be smart, productive workers who don't have feelings because feelings are stupid and get in the way of being "normal" and productive; and you will be happy about it.

Not to mention that these mothers were born during times of global trauma, including a pandemic, world wars, ongoing racism, the Holocaust, and more.

Some of these mothers then unwittingly passed the trauma (which at its core is a disconnection from one's feeling/sensing self) and shame to their daughters, even though many of them consciously intended not to do so.

As a result, some of their daughters chose to undo that conditioning and to walk a different path. They chose a different way to be women, a different way to be human, a different way to be mothers, a different way that might include not becoming a mother, a different way of mothering, a different way of working, a different way of relating, a different way of healing, a different way of life, a different way of [fill in the blank].

And instead of being okay with their daughters choosing a different way, some of those mothers take it as a personal affront and rebuke of themselves, their values, and their mothering. When uncomfortable feelings (usually fear, shame, or grief) arise, they don't have a healthy way to process those emotions (because they were taught not to). In some cases, those feelings are so painful they trigger a fight, flight, freeze, appease (or fawn) response.

If your mother is one of those mothers, when you try to talk with her about it, you're met with some combination of a blank stare, tears, dismissive comments, helplessness, pity, resentment, contempt, anger, and definitely a lack of empathy.

The vulnerability is too much.

She "can't" have these conversations. She can't acknowledge her own trauma or choose to do her own healing work because her nervous system has been hijacked, and even though the tools are now available to her too, she won't use them.

Over time, she created a narcissistic shield to protect herself from the shame, fear, and deep sadness or grief. She became increasingly bitter, critical, and negative, and she projects the shame, fear, and sadness onto you. This can create a trauma bond between the two of you.

As you grow (and do your own inner work, which your mother may criticize you for), you may find it increasingly hard to be around your mother. You may realize that you don't feel safe around her, that it takes too much energy to "control" yourself around her. It can be hard to like and respect yourself around her if this dynamic is in operation.

You want to break the trauma bond—break the cycle. And the more you separate in this way, the more autonomous you become, the more angry, hurt, sad, jealous, and resentful your mother could become.

> **"Resenting your daughter won't halt her progress."**
>
> **—paraphrased from Marshall McLuhan, who said it about technology**

You then have a heart-wrenching choice: attachment (no matter how insecure) to your mother, and maybe also holding onto a sense of belonging in your family of origin, or your own authenticity and aliveness.

My sense is that it's rare for an adult daughter, who is enmeshed (through no fault of her own) with a mother such as I describe above, to be able to choose her own authenticity and aliveness without going no-contact, at least for a little while.

It's possible for an adult daughter, who has gone no-contact and has done her own work to cultivate and protect her authenticity and aliveness, to reestablish contact with her mother in a healthy way, with new boundaries.

It's also possible for an adult daughter who has chosen permanent estrangement from her mother to live a life of authenticity and aliveness, no matter what people assume about her.

Estrangement isn't the shameful disease, but it can be the medicine.

You are not your mother.

You are not your mother's unrepaired trauma.

You are not her unexamined shame.

You are not her criticisms, biases, and judgment.

> **"Generational trauma is trauma that isn't just experienced by one person—it extends from one generation to the next. It can be silent, covert, and undefined, surfacing through nuances and inadvertently taught or implied throughout someone's life from an early age onward."**
> **—Melanie English, PhD**

CHAPTER 4

SHAME IS LIKE AN APPENDIX

There may, at one time in the very distant past, have been a healthy reason or "positive" purpose for humans to experience shame.

The same can be said for an appendix.

According to evolutionary biologists, at one time humans needed an appendix to digest food. It is no longer needed for that purpose. And yet humans are still born with an appendix—an organ that can make them sick and maybe even kill them. That is why they are often removed. At some point the human body will evolve to the point where it doesn't have an appendix.

According to evolutionary psychologists, shame evolved to serve a function of social defense, similar to the way pain protects us from things that hurt us physically. We are born with shame "hardwired" into our physiology. It is no longer needed for that purpose, and yet we still experience it. And it can make us sick and, in some cases, kill us.

In other words, there is no longer such a thing as "healthy" shame.

There are people who believe shame is "needed" in order to be "good." That's what guilt is for.

Shame = I am bad. Irredeemably bad. There's no coming back from this.

Guilt = I did something that is out of alignment with my values or my own moral code, and now I will course-correct.

There is never, ever, ever a good or healthy reason to believe you are bad.

Yet if you *do* believe it, it's not your fault. Most of us think shame is reserved for when you do something truly terrible and you feel like a bad person.

But here's the thing: Most of us have grown up learning that there is a right way and a wrong way to do everything, and if you choose the wrong way, you've made a bad choice or decision, and that means you're a bad person.

What's actually true is that most decisions and choices in life are morally neutral.

You don't need shame to keep you in line.

Shame won't hold you accountable.

Shame won't "rehabilitate" you.

Shame isn't what keeps you in integrity.

Connection to yourself and what you value does that.

Empathy and self-accountability do that.

You don't need shame.

Your will never shame yourself to goodness or wholeness.

If ever there was a hill to die on, it's this one. Besides...

> **"I'd rather be whole than good."**
> —Carl Jung

CHAPTER 5

THE THING YOU MIGHT FEEL THE MOST SHAME ABOUT TURNS OUT TO BE ONE OF THE MOST INTELLIGENT THINGS ABOUT YOU

You may have been brought up with the idea that your feelings and emotions are inconvenient, not important, or maybe even detrimental.

In fact, a Nobel prize-winning psychologist named Herb Simon, who worked in the 1960s and '70s, suggested that emotions "disrupt" cognitive function.

This premise continues on today despite research that indicates it's not true.

I learned this while listening to an episode of *On Being with Krista Tippett* in which she interviews neuroscientist Richard Davidson, the William James and Vilas Research Professor of Psychology and Psychiatry at the University of Wisconsin-Madison. He also founded and directs the Center for Healthy Minds and was the founding director of the Waisman Brain Imaging Lab.

This explains why many of us were taught to discount our feelings and/or maybe even to be ashamed of them.

What we know now is that feelings (or sensations) and emotions are what make your body intelligent.

———

Of all the things I was taught to be ashamed of, the most harmful was being made to believe that my body's intelligence was shameful. I was taught that the way my body deals with perceived threats and dangers is silly. Pathetic. Weak. Ineffectual.

And that's because my body, when presented with a perceived threat, tends to freeze. I shut down. I become a deer-in-the-headlights. Conflict-avoidant.

"Just like your father," my mother would say. She made it no secret that she didn't like or respect him.

My mother's body, on the other hand, when presented with a perceived threat, tends to fight. She becomes aggressive, mean, and angry.

Neither one is right or wrong (although my mother would disagree).

———

It's the day before my fifty-seventh birthday. I am driving home from a storytelling workshop and hear part of an interview with Saeed Jones, author of *How We Fight for Our Lives*, which is about growing up Black and gay in Texas in the 1990s.

He talks about how he erased himself in order to have a good relationship with his mother. He said that they could talk about anything except him being gay, and so he prioritized his mother's feelings over his own because he loved her and because he didn't want to cause her pain by trying to talk about it. And still, he said, she was his mom, and he needed to have her wisdom in terms of love and relationships. He didn't get that from her, and he really struggled as a result.

I think about the ways I have erased parts of myself, not just with my mother, but with others as well.

Later, my mother calls to wish me a happy birthday.

"How old are you now? Fifty-seven?" she asks.

"Yeah, can you believe it?" I reply.

"I can't believe I'm going to be eighty next year," she says. "I really don't feel eighty."

"And I don't feel fifty-seven."

The conversation follows the path it normally does: the weather, how her husband is doing, her bridge games.

I take a deep breath and decide to share something about me... something I would normally "erase" for her.

"I went to New York City last week—"

"New York City?!" she exclaims with a tone I label as a combination of suspicious and aggressive.

"Yes, I went for a workshop—"

"A workshop?? What kind of workshop?" Her tone ratchets up.

"It was about unpacking your biases—"

"Pfft. Well, did you unpack them?" This time I hear sarcasm.

"Yep," I reply, and then rush into the next subject. "And the day before, I saw my friend Suzanne, who worked at *Chemical Engineering* magazine when I worked at *Modern Plastics*. She came to our wedding, remember? I haven't seen her in more than twenty years."

"I don't remember her. Does she still work for *Chemical Engineering*?"

"No, she freelances as a technical writer for the chemical and pharmaceutical industries."

"Oh, I enjoy reading those kinds of articles... Do you still write?" she asks.

"Yes! I have two books coming out next year."

"What are they about?"

"One of them is a guided journal for mothers and daughters, and the other one is about creativity and overcoming your inner critic."

"And these books sell?" she asks, tone still intact, plus a hint of incredulousness (my interpretation).

I laugh. "I don't think my publisher would continue to ask me to write books if they didn't sell."

With each back-and-forth of the conversation, I feel my nervous system responding. My heart is beating faster, my breathing becomes more shallow, and my limbs feel weak. I am having what Pete Walker, therapist and author of *Complex PTSD: From Surviving to Thriving*, calls an emotional flashback. I am starting to dissociate and "freeze."

I wrap it up pretty quickly after that.

Later, I joke with my husband that the theme from *Jaws* would have been an appropriate soundtrack for the conversation.

Then I have a significant moment of clarity.

If my nervous system perceives the conversation as dangerous, then it's possible (probable?) that my mother's nervous system also perceives danger. Our authentic selves weren't having the conversation, our triggered nervous systems were.

As long as the conversation is "safe," it's fine. But when we enter "dangerous" territory, my nervous system wants to flee or freeze, and her nervous system wants to fight. (Again, Walker's book sheds so much light on this, and based on stories my mother has told me about her growing up years, it would not surprise me if "fight" is her nervous system's default mode.)

This doesn't make either of us bad or wrong, it's simply how we learned to survive. It's what happens when the ancient parts of our brains perceive danger, whether we're actually in danger or not.

If this is you, remember that as an adult daughter, you can choose to have superficial conversations with your mother and not see it as a bad thing or a sad thing.

You can do your best not to trigger your nervous system or hers. This is an act of kindness. And you can acknowledge that you are not responsible for her or her nervous system.

You can remind yourself not to take your mother's words and tone of voice personally, while also knowing that your body can't perceive that kind of nuance.

There will be times when you're awkward or uncomfortable, times when you feel prickles of annoyance, and times when you feel grief (and myriad other emotions).

As an adult daughter, you can acknowledge your humanity—and hers.

As an adult daughter, you can establish healthy boundaries. You can gracefully end phone calls. You can choose not to answer calls. You can choose to visit or not. You can define the parameters of your interactions.

Without a lot of drama.

Without blame.

And without shame.

Because you are not your mother.

———

The things you may yearn to embody—self-trust, self-confidence, self-esteem, self-acceptance, self-love, and self-regard—can come from learning about your human nervous system, expanding its capacity or window of tolerance, and understanding how to work with it.

No matter how your body responds to a perceived threat, that response is above all else intelligent. It is wise. It's a sign of strength and adaptability.

Whether the threat is real or perceived doesn't matter.

Because your body's response is intended to save your life.

Your body's response is intended to save your life.

There's nothing more intelligent than that.

And there's nothing shameful about it.

———

While I do not align with any particular religion or consider myself religious, the more I work with shame and the nervous system, the more spiritual I become.

The closest I've come to a definition of God I can get behind is this one:

> **"God dwells within you, as you yourself, just the way you are."**
> —**Elizabeth Gilbert in her memoir,** *Eat, Pray, Love*

You are not separate or disconnected from whatever force was involved in creating you.

For years the personal development and spirituality community spoke of the "mind-body-spirit connection" as if they were separate things. Now neuroscience is showing us they are one and the same.

Getting back to that episode of *On Being* dealing with love, kindness, learning, and education, Davidson's work "illuminates the rich interplay between things we saw as separate not that long ago: body, mind, spirit, emotion, behavior, and genetics."

According to Davidson, "...the brain does not honor the kind of anachronistic distinction between thought and feeling. Thought and feeling are absolutely intermingled in the brain, and so there are no areas of the brain that are exclusively dedicated to one and not the other. There's a lot of interconnectivity. When a child, for example, is subjected to adversity, and the adversity gets under the skin, it will impair cognitive function in addition to producing emotional difficulties. These are intimately interwoven in the brain." (The above is from the *On Being with Krista Tippett* episode entitled, "Richard Davidson: A Neuroscientist on Love and Learning," February 2019)

The descriptive phrase "and the adversity gets under the skin" is to me another way of explaining how trauma and shame go together.

I'm guessing that one day, it will be proven with science that the human nervous system, with all its incredible and yet-to-be-fully-understood intelligence, is what connects to what some people call God. Maybe it's one and the same.

> **"Science and spirituality are two sides of the same coin, and we cannot separate one from the other."**
>
> **—Thomas Vazhakunnathu, spiritual scientist, teacher, and author**

PART III

THE PRACTICES

Right now, it's easy for your brain to offer you shame and for your body to experience it.

It's like a well-lit, smooth, and wide superhighway. It's easy to drive fast on it, and there are no speed traps or tolls to slow you down. (Your brain's superhighways are called *neural pathways*—they allow signals to travel from one part of the brain to another. Because brains like to be efficient, the more you use a particular superhighway, the smoother and faster it becomes, even if you're using it for something like shame.)

What you're about to do is take an exit off that superhighway and go to a deep, dark, tangled jungle with a machete and start hacking a path. It's going to be sweaty, hard work, and you may not have faith that anything else can take shame's place in your brain.

Because your brain has neural plasticity, you can build unshamed neural pathways. The adage that "Old dogs can't learn new tricks" is false.

I've done this. And having come out on the other side into the sunlight, I can fully and honestly say it's worth it.

You can't walk my path, but you can learn from observing me, and I will be cheering you on as you clear your own new path.

CHAPTER 6

GROWLING, PATTING, AND STOMPING

Because your human nervous system it is a major character in the story of your life, learning about it and learning how to work with it will play a major role in your unshaming journey because it will show you just how intelligent it—and you—are.

There are many, *many* comprehensive resources out there on trauma and the nervous system, and I will point you to some of them in the resource section, but this book wouldn't be complete without the basics.

There is a concept that comes from the field of chemistry which is applied in the field of trauma recovery called *titration*.

> **"Titration is the slow addition of one solution of a known concentration to a known volume of another solution of unknown concentration until the reaction reaches neutralization, which is often indicated by a color change."**
>
> **—LibreTexts: Chemistry**

In other words:

> **"Less is more; slower tends to be better; start with what's easy, move your attention to what's hard, then move back to what's easy."**
>
> —**Rachael Maddox**

Disclaimer: I am not a neuroscientist, psychologist, licensed trauma therapist, or physician. What I offer here is an overview and synthesis of what I have learned from studying, taking classes, and working with experts in the field. This information and the practices I share can be an effective companion to therapy, but they are not a replacement for it. If you are in therapy, you may want to share this information and these practices with your therapist.

The human central nervous system is comprised of the brain and the spinal cord.

The part of the nervous system that's important to understand when it comes to shame is the Autonomic Nervous System (ANS). The ANS controls your internal environment automatically. It works below your level of consciousness as a completely natural and organic system (*"shame doesn't knock"*).

Polyvagal Theory, introduced by behavioral neuroscientist Stephen W. Porges, PhD, posits that the ANS has three branches (ventral-vagal, sympathetic, and dorsal-vagal) that work together automatically, adjusting to cues of safety and danger. These cues can be from the external environment, from within your body, or simply from your perception. They are not "logical."

The ventral-vagal branch is the "safe" state. It is the healthy balance between your foot on the gas and your foot on the brake. In this state, you're relaxed and appropriately alert. You are grounded and connected. It's often referred to as the "safe and social" state. It's "here and now," and it's where you have agency and can make choices about who you want to be and what you want to do.

The sympathetic branch is the "mobilized" state. It could be considered your foot on the gas. When safe, it is your inhale, your muscle flexion, your get-up-and-go. Under threat, it is responsible for activation of the fight-or-flight response. It's a fast-and-racing state.

The dorsal-vagal branch is the "immobilized" state. It is your foot on the brake. When safe, it is your exhale, your ability to rest and digest, your ability to relax and let go. Under threat, it is responsible for activating freeze. A feigned death response is the extreme. It's a checked out and dejected state.

The dorsal-vagal branch is where shame lives.

While you can't choose your autonomic states, you can influence them. You can build "capacity" in your system. This means that you're able to "be with" what you are feeling and sensing in the moment. You are aware of what's happening inside you and can identify it and work with it.

When you're unaware, it's harder to navigate your body's fight, flight, freeze, and appease (or fawn) responses.

It's helpful to understand that your body may have a default or go-to response. As I described above, my body tends to default to the dorsal-vagal response of freeze. This doesn't mean the sympathetic branch of my nervous system is never activated, it's simply that my body learned that freeze is most likely to keep me safe and alive.

There are physical and emotional cues/clues for both the sympathetic and dorsal-vagal branches.

When the sympathetic branch is activated, you might notice irritation or annoyance at first. Then the sensations build to defensiveness, frustration, anger, and finally, full-on rage. Cortisol and adrenaline are released into the body to prepare you for either running away or putting up a fight. Blood flows away from your vital organs and into your limbs and extremities for the same reason.

Let's look at the four stress/survival responses: Fight, Flight, Freeze, and Appease (or fawn):

Fight = "Physically overcoming, injuring, or killing the threat will make me feel safe." In anger, you want to snarl, growl, glare, sneer, stomp, push, punch, scream, hit, kick, claw, or strangle. Your muscles, hands, and jaw become tense. Your heart rate increases. Your breathing becomes rapid and shallow and/or you hold your breath. Your vision narrows so you can focus on who or what you are fighting.

Flight = "Running away will make me safe." It feels like you need to get the hell out. Your mind races and you find it hard to sit still. There is an "I have to get this right" feeling. There is arousal in your limbs, shaking, trembling, twisting. There is an impulse to back up, flee, turn away. You might hold your breath or you may breathe rapidly. You may experience a sense of urgency, anxiety, or restlessness. Your pupils dilate and your eyes shift.

When the dorsal-vagal branch is activated, you might notice confusion at first, then disorientation, moving into helplessness and hopelessness, overwhelm, panic, shock, and then shutdown or collapse. This is when freeze happens.

Freeze = "Disappearing will make me safe." There is disorientation or dissociation; shrinking; hiding; a deer-in-the-headlights feeling; self-isolating; spacing out; self-soothing with sleep, scrolling, bingeing; or you blank out and can't think what to say. Your heart rate decreases, and your breathing becomes more shallow. You experience stiffness or heaviness in your limbs. You can't think straight or make decisions. Blood flows in toward your vital organs. At the extreme, this is "playing dead."

What the nervous system is trying to convey through freeze is, "I can't cope with what is present, internally and externally, and so I'll shut down, disappear, avoid, and disconnect."

Appeasing or fawning, which was first described by psychotherapist Pete Walker in his book *Complex PTSD: From Surviving to Thriving*, doesn't fall neatly into either the sympathetic or dorsal-vagal branches. It is a little bit of both.

Appease (or fawn) = "Putting my needs and wants aside and giving others what they want will make me safe." This is where people-pleasing happens. You agree with someone you disagree with, you apologize when there's nothing to apologize for, you say "yes" when you don't want to. You bend, contort, shape-shift, and hide your authentic self. It's the inability to say "no" or disagree. There is excessive concern about what others think. There is a fear of being seen or of taking up space. You detach from your needs and comfort in order to cater to others. This is where codependency is born.

Some definitions of trauma:

> **"Trauma is in the nervous system and body, and not in the event; an event that is very traumatic to one person may not be traumatic to another, as people differ very widely in their ability to handle various kinds of challenging situations due to different genetic makeup, early environmental challenges, and specific trauma and attachment histories."**
>
> **—Peter Levine, developer of Somatic Experiencing**

"Anything that was too much, too soon, or too fast for your nervous system to process and integrate."

—Unknown

"Any experience that made you feel unsafe in your fullest authentic expression and led to developing trauma adaptations to keep you safe."

—Valerie Rein, author of *Patriarchy Stress Disorder*

"Trauma isn't the bad, hurtful thing that happened. It's having to be alone with the hurt and it not being okay or safe to feel and process emotions associated with being hurt (anger, fear, sadness, shame). It's the disconnection from self/feeling."

—Dr. Gabor Maté

"Trauma is an unbearable experience that lacks a relational home. A relational home is a space where you feel safe enough to feel some of the overwhelming emotions of the event with someone else that can help you bear it."

—MaryCatherine McDonald, PhD

In addition to titrating, here are some other helpful concepts from the field of Somatic Experiencing®:

Resourcing: being attuned to sensations of safety or goodness, no matter how small, and then creating moments of safety and goodness on purpose to increase the amount of resource you have.

Pendulation: being aware of the natural back-and-forth between feelings of expansion and contraction, ebb and flow, alertness/action, and calm/rest. This helps develop confidence in the ability to move between states.

Neuroception: the ability to distinguish whether situations or people are safe, dangerous, or life-threatening.

Proprioception: your body's ability to perceive its own position in space. For example, proprioception enables you to close your eyes and touch your nose with your index finger.

Interoception: the ability to perceive how your body feels inside. It is a reference point for interpretations of connection, safety, and emotional states.

Exteroception: the ability to perceive a stimulus originating outside your body (light, sound, temperature, pressure).

Somatics: "soma" is Greek for body.

> **"Somatics are body-based practices where the mind-body is studied, explored, experienced, experimented with...**and **given the space to be felt, connected with, and understood."**
> —**Victoria Albina, NP, MPH**

There are many simple somatic practices that can help you *increase nervous system capacity* and help you move out of dorsal-vagal and sympathetic states back into the ventral-vagal state. Increasing your nervous system capacity means you become an expert at what you are sensing and feeling in any given moment, and that your body can be with and "hold" the sensations of activation.

In general, any type of movement up-regulates and is a good way to bring yourself out of a dorsal-vagal state. Cool or cold water does the same.

In general, breathing (with a slow and steady inhalation-to-exhalation ratio, or making your exhalation last longer than your inhalation) down-regulates and is a good way to bring yourself out of a sympathetic state. Warm or hot water does the same.

Here are two of my favorites for working with shame:

This Is Mine/That's Not Mine: Cross your arms in front of you and alternate patting your hands on the opposite upper arms and shoulders. As you pat, say out loud, "This is mine...this is my body!" Then hold your arms out in front of you, palms up, facing away from you, and say, "That's not mine!" Your precious body is yours. The shame is not yours.

Access Your Inner Mama Bear: Growl. Bare your teeth. Make clawing motions with your hands (with gracious thanks to Kimberly Johnson, who shared this in one of her Jaguar classes). Stomp your feet. Hum or chant or sing. Rock or sway. Use your fists to lightly pound your solar plexus (not too hard) and go "ahhhhh."

Notice how you feel after doing these practices once or twice. Use the Somatic Experiencing® concepts above to track what's happening in your body. Stop if you don't like it. Exaggerate the movements. Make them smaller. Play. Notice.

Remind yourself:

- *I am safe and I've got my own back.*
- *I am an adult with agency.*
- *This is my body's response, and there's nothing wrong with it or me.*
- *This is my body's intelligence.*
- *I love and accept myself in this moment.*
- *How human of me.*
- *I am not my mother.*

———

How do you know you are experiencing shame?

Where does it live in your body?

What are the sensations?

What are the qualities?

What does your body do, or want to do, when you experience shame?

Do you want to hide? Do you want to run away? Do you want to punch and kick? Do you find yourself looking for approval and validation outside yourself?

Track your shame in your body. How do you know you're experiencing shame? Where does it start in your body? Where does it go? What happens to it? What happens to you?

Here's what looks and feels like for me.

Shame seems to come out nowhere and park itself on my solar plexus like a heavy flat rock. Just like Stephen King said, it doesn't knock.

My face prickles with heat.

I can't swallow.

My vision narrows.

I feel a dropping sensation.

I freeze.

I can't access my words.

It has me finding evidence all over the place for how I am—truly—a bad-to-the-bone person.

It has me wondering if anyone could possibly feel as much shame as I do, and then I tell myself, "No, of course not, because no one is as bad as I am."

My body crumples in on itself. I want to hide. I often cry. At the extreme, I send myself to my room and curl up in bed and sob like an inconsolable child. I can't accept comforting. I believe I am not fit to be around other people.

Sometimes it's more subtle. Sometimes it shows up as self-deprecating humor and eye rolls at myself. I call this micro-shame.

CHAPTER 7

IDENTIFY TIMES IN YOUR LIFE WHEN YOU EXPERIENCED SHAME

Whether she intended to or not (and I am pretty sure she didn't), your mother took the shame she internalized and handed it right to you.

Your stories, especially those from your childhood, are a great place to look for the genesis of shame-based thoughts and beliefs.

You can do this on your own, or you can ask a trusted friend, therapist, or coach to have a conversation with you. Tell them that you want to uncover and identify the thoughts and beliefs you have about yourself that cause you to experience shame.

Tell them not to interrupt or to try and fix it for you. Ask them to just simply listen with empathy (rather than pity or sympathy).

> **"Shame thrives when we are isolated, alone, and believe that no one else could possibly understand us or feel what we are feeling. One antidote is to reach out, connect, and talk about it to someone who will listen and empathize."**
>
> **—Brené Brown**

As I did in my Timeline of Disconnection, Trauma, and Shame, write down as many details as you can, and don't censor yourself. What happened? Who was there? What do you remember? What are the beliefs you internalized? What did you make these instances mean about you?

CHAPTER 8

CARRY IT WITH YOU

You will probably not be able to banish those thoughts and beliefs forever.

It's likely that the computer-in-your-head will continue to offer those thoughts to you.

You may never completely replace them with other thoughts.

Even though you might try.

So for now, carry them with you, but outside of you.

Consciously.

Do not burn them.

Do not shred them.

Do not bury them.

Do not ignore them.

There's so much relief here.

When you identify those shame-based thoughts, it's tempting to believe you can just get rid of them or "positive affirmation" them away. This often leads to what I call meta-shame, or shame about your shame.

"There must be something REALLY wrong with me if I can't stop this shame!"

Because you can't just turn those thoughts off.

This part of the process is designed to help you get some space and perspective.

Write your shame-based thoughts and beliefs out on little pieces of paper, fold them up, and put them in a small box. A small jewelry box will do. You can decorate it or not.

Carry the box with you or put it in a place where you will see it and its contents often.

Now you can see that they are no longer unconsciously internalized, and while you may never completely rid yourself of them...that's okay.

I've had mine ("I'm bad," "I'm a selfish, spoiled brat," and "I'm a pathetic loser") sitting in a small, cardboard box on my desk for about three years, and I relate to them very differently now than I did before.

When I am able to catch my brain trying to offer me one of my shame-based thoughts, I say to myself, "This is the part where my brain tries to offer me shame. And this is the part where I decline and say, No thank you! It's not mine!"

CHAPTER 9

TURN YOUR INNER SHAMER INTO A CARICATURE[1]

I'm in a room with a bunch of other women, all of whom are impeccably dressed. They are intellectual, calm, confident, learned...smooth.

And me? I'm slightly sweaty, my hair is frizzy and unkempt, and my clothes don't fit well. Sloppy. Chunky. Awkward. Desperate.

When they see me, they chuckle to each other. I see them side-eyeing me as they cover their mouths and whisper to each other:

"Isn't she cute...she thinks she's making a contribution."

I approach them, and try to speak.

They "tut-tut" and roll their eyes.

They fake-smile at me with pity in their eyes. With a flick of their hands, they say, "Run along now."

I'm dismissed, seen as irrelevant, out-of-step, "lite," naive, not thorough enough, fluffy, silly, too little too late. Inadequate on all counts.

If I had to choose their representative it would be the one and only Patsy Stone, from the British TV show *Absolutely Fabulous*.

---

1   A picture, description, or imitation of a person in which certain striking characteristics are exaggerated in order to create a comic or grotesque effect.

She is the embodiment of my Inner Shamer.

Who is your Inner Shamer?

Where did he/she/it/they come from?

Is the voice that of a specific person from your past?

Or a combination of people?

Draw a picture, literally or with words, of this person. Get really specific about what they look like and how they act. Do they have a name? What is it? Describe their voice.

CHAPTER 10

IDENTIFY AND BE
YOUR FAVORITE SELF

Unshaming is not about being your best, highest, most organized, or most productive self, but being your favorite self.

When I am being my favorite self, I am:

- mischievous. And I have to look that word up every time because I can't spell it. I always spell it like this: mischevious, pronounced like "devious."

- hiding in closets waiting for my husband to walk by so I can jump out and scare him, but usually I start laughing before I can surprise him. I literally have to hold my hand over my mouth, but it doesn't always work. That, or I feel like I have to pee.

- crying with a coaching client, because if crying with a client is wrong, I don't want to be right.

- running around the kitchen island with my dog Scout's toy and she is chasing me (or vice versa).

- a goofball.

- writing the way I like and want to write, not the way I think I should write. (And guess what? For a while, I was writing this book the way I thought I should...not the way I like and want to express myself.)

- welling up with tender tears over something I heard or read.

- inappropriately laughing in a situation that does not call for it, like on the occasion a very long time ago when my father, stepmother, half sister and brother and I had Thanksgiving dinner at some fancy-schmancy restaurant in North Conway, New Hampshire, and something was said that was so funny that before we knew it, we were laughing so hard we couldn't speak and tears were running down our faces, and people were looking at us and that just made us laugh even harder.

- talking back to a recipe and saying "I don't think so" and then taking the easy way out.

- whispering *"me too"* when a potential client tells me she sometimes wishes her mother were dead (knowing that my mother used to sometimes wish the same thing about *her* mother).

- telling a story that makes people's eyes widen and their skin get goosebumps.

- ...helping someone have an *aha* moment that will change their life forever. I might be pounding my palms against my desk.

Who are you when you're being your favorite self? Not your most evolved self. Not your "best" self. Not your "higher" self. Your *favorite* self.

CHAPTER 11

GIVE YOUR
SELF-CONCEPT AN
UNSHAMED UPDATE

You may not be able to fully eliminate your shame-based thoughts, but you can create new ones that will become stronger than your shame-based thoughts. You will start to relate to your shame-based thoughts differently. They won't knock as hard as they used to.

Your "self-concept" is the collection of thoughts and beliefs you hold about yourself. It's who you think you are—your identity. The term comes from the field of psychology.

In addition to "I'm a pathetic loser," which has been part of my self-concept since I was a pre-teen, "I'm a writer" has also been part of my self-concept since then. For many years, "pathetic loser" was stronger than "writer."

I didn't really start expressing myself via writing until shame started to lose its grip on me. Without realizing it, I started thinking, "I have something to say, and the way I say it matters because it helps me explain myself to myself. And it appears that when I do that, I help other people understand themselves." (Thank you Pat Conroy!)

Creating and cultivating identity is a significant part of the unshaming process because, whether you're aware of it or not, who you *believe yourself to be* impacts your sense of purpose.

And if you're a woman or someone socialized as a woman who has shame at your core, this becomes the foundation of being able to understand yourself. When you are equipped with a sense of identity, you will be able to figure out and cultivate what your purpose is in the world, beyond what you were socialized to believe your purpose ought to be.

Because shame makes it hard to clearly see, know, and trust yourself, focusing on and intentionally cultivating traits, qualities, and values you admire helps.

This exercise will help you tap into what you value and remind yourself of who you are and what's actually true about you.

> **I created this exercise by combining concepts I learned from Brooke Castillo at the Life Coach School, Randi Buckley, who teaches the Healthy Boundaries for Kind People approach, and Tanya Geisler, a leadership coach who specializes in impostor complex.**

For this practice, you are going to think back to four different types of moments in your life:

1. **Times when you felt alive and energized, in the zone, or authentically you in all your you-ness.**

2. **Times when you felt in awe, tender, or moved to tears, in the best possible way.**

3. **Times when you felt compelled to take action and/or step in to protect, when you felt righteous anger or that your sense of justice and fairness had been transgressed.**

4. **Times when you felt a sense of deep respect or dignity.**

As you picture each of these moments, summon the emotional and sensory experience of that moment and the sensations you felt in your body.

You can do this on your own, or you can ask a trusted friend, therapist, or coach to have a conversation with you. Tell them that you want to tell them about powerful, wonderful times in your life.

What were you doing? Who were you with? What else was happening? What did you believe and feel? Immerse yourself in that moment, giving attention to all your senses, and describe what it was like in as much detail as possible.

Give each moment a name: a word or phrase that sums up each experience.

Those words or phrases are antidotes to shame. They are the summation of multisensory, emotional experiences you liked having. Landing on those words or phrases might feel like a puzzle piece clicking into place. They might feel like a zing or a tingle. They might feel like warmth. They might feel expansive. They might feel like a "knowing." They may have colors associated with them.

_____

I am standing on the Listen To Your Mother stage in the auditorium of the Providence Public Library in Providence, Rhode Island. I am about to read a personal essay I wrote that will eventually be published in *O Magazine*.

I hear the hush as I approach the microphone. There are people who love and support me in the audience.

With me on stage are the other women who were chosen to participate in this production, an event that has grown to encompass more than fifty cities across North America.

The air is still. It is quiet. I can feel my heart beating. I'm nervous and excited. My voice is clear although my hands are shaking.

I finish. There's a brief moment of silence. Then...loud applause! My heart is bursting with pride and love. Being able to use my voice in this way feels like coming home to myself.

Because when I was a child, I dreamed of standing on a stage in a fabulous dress and being able to sing a song that gave people goosebumps. As it turns out, singing is not my thing, but storytelling is.

Later, I am approached by people I know and people I don't know who thank me for my vulnerability and honesty.

In that moment (and even now as I write this), I feel Elemental Power. That is what I call my Unshamed Self-Concept.

———

Now spend a little more time thinking about and feeling into your experiences. What was in that recollection, and what tends to show up when you're experiencing those kinds of moments? What values or qualities are alive when you feel that feeling?

These moments and the values, qualities, or traits present in them are resources that will help you on your unshaming journey.

———

What was present for me in that moment on the Listen To Your Mother stage? After some reflection, I came up with three words. They are values and traits that are important to me always, in everything I do: Dignity. Expression. Audacity.

In fact, the energy of these three words is infused throughout this book.

Each has its own felt sense and bodily awareness. Just as shame is an experience, each of these three words is an experience.

Dignity feels like a steady, expansive certainty in my core and solar plexus. It includes deep respect.

Expression feels like a warm, silky, shimmering, golden flow in my chest and throat. It includes moments of awe and moments when I was moved to tears.

Audacity feels like an energized knowing, an expansive pulse throughout my body. It combines the moments of being in the zone and moments of righteous anger.

———

Now, identify how it feels in your body when you experience the values, traits, or qualities you chose. Think of sensations, temperatures, movements, textures, and so on, and where you feel them...in which body parts or areas?

Each of your four sets of moments has a series of thoughts, phrases, sayings, images, or memories attached to them.

When I want to remember who I am, when I want to stop a shame spiral, when I want to do something hard, when I want to show up a certain way in my relationships, I turn to one of my three pillars.

The most important part is that each pillar has a distinct felt sense that I like having and that I know I can tap into by remembering a story, an Image, or a thought.

Dignity, expression, and audacity: Each feels distinctly different in my body, and each serves me in different ways.

When I am working with a client on this, it's in the telling of their stories that they use words, phrases, and sentences that I can tell move them...and when that happens, I tell them to pay attention to what's happening in their bodies.

It's not about repeating someone else's thoughts or choosing thoughts because you think they "should" feel good in your body (although I borrow from others because their words land in my body in a way that I like).

It's about paying attention to what you already have inside and giving it language.

So, then, each pillar has its own set of thoughts, images, memories.

Then we create a way to remember.

I have decals of the words "Dignity. Expression. Audacity." on the wall above my computer monitor.

I also have it written down, and I keep it on my desk next to my box of shame.

Create an Unshamed Self-Concept vision board. Get a piece of jewelry that represents your Unshamed Self-Concept (or that represents your three pillars). Make an altar to it, a screen saver, or something else.

> **"You build belief through faithful intention."**
> —Christie Inge

It's a living, breathing practice. I've been doing it for five years, and it is ever evolving.

Dignity

Respect is my bottom line.

No one speaks to me that way.

Dear God, show me the truth about myself, no matter how beautiful it is (thank you, Macrina Wiederkehr).

Clear is kind.

I take my time.

How human of me.

I have nothing to explain, defend, prove, or hide (thank you, Lisa Nichols).

Expression

I write beautiful things.

I stand on my stories.

I am more committed to my work than I am afraid of feeling shame.

No one thinks like me.

I pour myself into my work, this is how I know myself.

I show up, do my thing, and leave it all on the stage or page.

Audacity

I am an extension of the power that created the entire universe (thank you, RuPaul).

This is just how it is when I show up.

I do it my way.

I don't have shit to prove.

F*ck yeah!

Rockstar!

CHAPTER 12

DON'T LOOK INTO DISTORTED MIRRORS, DO THIS INSTEAD

Sometimes your mother or someone else holds up a metaphorical mirror and you look into it not knowing that it is distorted with shame.

This is because people who are unaware of their shame tend to project it onto others. I have done this myself, many times.

It's important to know who these people are, and it's important not to trust what you see when you look into the mirrors they hold up.

When you're little and the person holding up the mirror is your mother, you can't do anything about it.

But once you're aware, you can say "no thank you" when she offers you her shame mirror. If every time you look into one of these mirrors, it feels terrible—like a big *ouch*—this is a signal.

And speaking of mirrors...

> **"Does your face light up?"**
>
> —Toni Morrison

She was talking to Oprah Winfrey and other readers of her novel, *The Bluest Eye*, during an Oprah Book Club discussion.

"When a kid walks in a room—your child or anyone else's child—does your face light up? Or do they see your critical face?"

The next time you catch a glimpse of yourself in the mirror, you don't have to say anything.

Just light up your face at your self, genuinely, as if you were greeting a child, and notice how it feels.

CHAPTER 13

YOU ARE NOT YOUR MOTHER (BUT YOU ARE LIKE HER... SOMETIMES...AND HERE'S HOW YOU'RE DIFFERENT)

Sometimes what's true is that the ways you are like your mother are "frowned upon in society."

In these instances, being like her isn't the problem, society is.

Choosing to be proud of the ways you're like your mother goes along with being discerning and intentional about the ways you don't want to be like her.

Because if you're afraid of being like your mother...

...it might be because you judge her.

Judgment is a normal human behavior, and it's one that is necessary.

You can decide you want to parent differently than your mother did or be different in other ways, but consider that what you *really* want is to be *free* in ways your mother wasn't.

You might really want to not beat yourself up like your mother might have beaten herself up.

You might really want not to feel compelled to drive yourself into the ground like your mother might have driven herself into the ground.

You might really want not to be reactive and defensive like your mother might be reactive and defensive.

It's likely that your mother is and was living and parenting with the same (or similar) internalized shame-based thoughts like "I'm unworthy" and "I'm not important."

Thoughts she believed without questioning, which became her identity, and from which all of her behavior flowed.

She might be tough and prickly.

She might be a shrinking violet.

She might be a people pleaser, putting everyone else ahead of herself.

She might be a passive-aggressive manipulator.

Believe it or not, all of these personas can come from the same basic belief of "I'm not good enough."

So when you find yourself thinking, *"Oh my God, am I just like my mother? SHIT...I am!"*

And you experience shame...

This is where you can interrupt the pattern...

This is where you get to choose to do it differently.

You do this not by being different than—or the opposite of—your mother, but by revealing those painful beliefs you have about yourself, by reckoning with those uncomfortable feelings, and ultimately by healing them.

Your life and your health are too precious to spend another moment, hour, day, week, month, year, or decade stuck in generational patterns not of your choosing.

Because you are not your mother.

CHAPTER 14

CULTIVATING ANGER IN SERVICE TO DIGNITY, HONOR, AND INTEGRITY

Shaming works because it calls your sense of dignity, honor, and integrity into question.

Because shame distorts the way you see yourself, it also distorts your ability to trust your anger, as well as your other emotions.

Even if it feels like you've never had any dignity, honor, and integrity, I can assure you that you do. You wouldn't be seeking out ways to unshame yourself if you had no dignity, honor, and integrity.

One way to uncover these qualities within you is to recall times when you liked and respected yourself and the reasons you did something. Make a list of those times.

I once worked with a client who experiences shame when she feels and/or expresses anger and when she, in her own words, "overreacts."

Shame is an emotion, and it is a secondary sensory response to how she experiences herself as someone who feels and expresses anger.

Many of us experience shame when we feel or express anger because somewhere along the line, we learned that anger isn't okay for us...or that it won't be the thing that protects us and keeps us alive.

It's dangerous.
It's "unbecoming."

It's "not feminine."
It can get us locked up.
It can get us kicked out.
It can get us killed.

When I asked my client if she could remember a time when a trusted adult might have praised her in a scenario where she expressed anger, she told me that when she was in elementary school, there was an older, bigger girl who was bullying little kids on the school bus.

One day, she decided to confront the bully. She told the bully to *stop it!!*

The bully retorted, "Make me!"

So she got up and hit the bully.

(Watching her energy change as she told the story was priceless.)
Then she said that she knew she would get in trouble, but that it was okay because she was defending someone else.

When the bus arrived at her stop, the bus driver escorted her to her front door and told her mother what had happened, and that, as a "punishment," he was going to make her sit in the seat directly behind him for a month.

"I could tell that the bus driver was actually proud of me for standing up to the bully," she told me, "and I didn't see having to sit behind him as a punishment. Yes, I was being held accountable for hitting the bully, but in that month of sitting behind the bus driver, he let me know that he thought I was brave...a good kid."

When shame takes root, it's hard to see what's true about you.

You need to rely on the truth that a compassionate witness can reflect back to you.

Despite the shaming she received from her mother, and then internalized, she now has a resource: that bus driver's wisdom. She has a memory and an experience that she can viscerally feel and count on. It lives within her.

Her stories and memories and imagination are a resource. They are rich with thoughts, images, emotions, sensations, and even movements.

And so are yours.

Trigger warning for the following page:
This childhood recollection briefly describes an incident
of animal torture by another person.

Her story reminded me of the time, when I was about twelve, that I saw a boy putting a frog into wet cement that was being poured for a sidewalk in my neighborhood.

The frog couldn't escape, and the boy was using a cigarette to burn its eyes. I can barely write about it without feeling the swell of horror and intense anger mixed with sadness (or grief?) in my chest.

I picked up a rock and threw it at his head and ran.

He never saw me coming and he ended up with a concussion.

Just like my client who knew it was wrong to hit the other girl on the school bus, I know it was wrong to throw a rock at that boy.

But I also love and admire my justice-minded twelve-year-old-self who couldn't abide animal torture (and who still can't) and who did what she saw as an honorable thing.

You are probably someone who is quick to defend and protect others.

And you may find it more difficult to do the same for yourself.

Notice when you're not standing up for yourself—when you're not defending and protecting your own dignity, honor, and integrity—because you don't believe you deserve it, or because you've internalized the shame that comes from not having had a compassionate witness when your dignity, honor, and integrity were attacked or called into question.

Then ask yourself what it would look like to stand up for yourself. What would it take for you to believe you deserve to protect your dignity, honor, and integrity?

There's a difference between the anger you feel when you believe you don't deserve respect and the anger you feel when you are being treated disrespectfully *and* you know you are worthy of dignity and self-respect.

The first kind of anger tends to be explosive, volcanic, long-lasting. You stoke it and ruminate over it and ultimately feel powerless with it.

The second kind, the anger that emerges when you know your own worth, tends to be fast and clean-burning. You know what to do with it. It's *No!* or *Stop it!* Or, it's a turning away...a withdrawing of your energy from that person.

It's a subtle, but important difference.

This is what unshamed anger looks like.

There is nothing wrong with withdrawing your energy from others.

And there's nothing wrong with wielding your anger when necessary—as you explore what it's like to act from that fast, clean-burning anger.

> **"Your anger is a part of you that loves you."**
> **—Lyndsey Gallant**

You get to choose in any given moment.

> **"Righteous anger is a fast, hot fire that burns up the poison of shaming and protects your field of honor. This is the anger that rises up like a dragon and says, 'No one speaks to me that way!' This anger is correct and just and fair. You are entitled to it. You must claim it."**
>
> **—Dr. Mario Martinez, author of The Mind-Body Code**

Remember, it's not just that someone hurt or harshly judged or criticized you, it's that you didn't have a compassionate witness. Righteous anger protects you from judging yourself when others try to shame you.

I spent decades of my life unable to trust my anger. I would enter into what I call a fury-devastation-shame spiral when being mistreated, especially by my mother.

———

My husband and I visit my mother for a few days.

I leave to do some work.

She asks my husband why I have to work when I am visiting. He tells her how proud he is of me, how successful he thinks I am, how he sees that I help so many people.

Later, he tells me about their conversation and says that she seemed to be in disbelief, that she wanted to contradict what he was saying about me.

I reply, "My perception is that it's hard for her to have her opinion of me challenged. And one of her opinions of me (again, this is my perception) is that I am a weak and ineffectual person."

Later still, when we are all together again, she tells the story of how, when I was an infant with a fever of a 106, the doctor told her to put me in a cold bath so I wouldn't get brain damage.

"I guess it didn't work," she says, looking at me to gauge my reaction.

I don't respond. No one does.

"Just kidding," she says. "Ha ha ha."

She goes on to tell more stories about how I am just like my father. (She has made it clear many times over the years that she didn't like or respect him.)

It's almost as if she has to restore her story about me and knock me down a few pegs in the face of conflicting evidence.

> **"The way you see any individual in your mind is the best they can ever be in your presence."**
> **—John Overdurf**

The whole thing reminds me of the way her father used to recount the story of how she "flunked out of college after her freshman year because she majored in bridge and boys."

Ha ha ha.

I remember the last time I heard my grandfather say that to her. It was in a room full of family, including her then new husband and his son.

I remember finding her upstairs in her bedroom later, crying.

I remember her saying how much she wanted her father's attention and approval.

I remember trying to make her feel better.

I remember times in my life when I leaned on the bruises of
people I love.

———

I am hurt because I am a human who is sensitive to cruelty.

I am angry because I no longer allow myself to be shamed.

I trust myself and my responses and my experiences. I don't
gaslight myself.

I say *ouch* when it hurts.

And I decide what to do about it.

In that quiet moment after her "ha ha ha," I shift my energy away from
her. I keep my body turned slightly away. I am cool.

———

On the car ride home, I cry.

I grieve for my loss of a mother who might see me as I am, and I grieve
her loss of a father (and mother) who might have seen her as she is.

———

It's not about taking a cruel "joke" personally.

It's about holding myself in such high regard that I remove myself from
cruel and abusive situations in a way that serves me.

It's about cultivating, on purpose, my identity—the way I want to think
about myself in regard to this situation.

I respect the way I handle myself.

It serves me to respond the way I did.

I am so proud of myself.

It's okay to take things personally.

Being sensitive isn't a problem.

It's only painful when I think it shouldn't be.

I tend to "overreact" when I think I have to defend who I am.

"Honor will inevitably overwhelm shame."

—Dr. Mario Martinez

Apply dignity liberally.

Add a layer of compassion.

Remember yourself.

Commit to yourself.

Be loyal to yourself.

Sprinkle it all with self-trust and patience, and serve it with a side of inner growl.

CHAPTER 15

FIND & CREATE RESOURCES

Being attuned, aware, and receptive to sensations of safety or moments of goodness, no matter how small, and then creating moments of safety and goodness on purpose will increase the amount of resources you have.

There's a photo of former New Zealand Prime Minister Jacinda Ardern wrapping her arms around one of the survivors of the Christchurch mosque shooting.

Her arms are fully around this other human. Her cheek pressed against the cheek of this person. Her eyes are closed.

I am moved to tears every time I see it. I keep it close so I can see it when I want to feel this way, to be reminded that if I can feel so deeply by looking at a photograph, that deep unconditional love exists within me.

It's not out there.

It's in here.

———

Place your hands on your own face.

Place your hands over your own heart.

You don't have to be any different than you are right in this very moment in order to feel and receive love.

———

I didn't watch the 2022 Oscars, but I heard about a moment (not that moment).

Liza Minnelli and Lady Gaga appear on stage to present the Best Picture Oscar.

Liza appears to stumble over her words, and Gaga leans over and quietly says, "I got you," and Liza replies, "I know."

Because they had "hot" mics, we get to hear this tender and loving exchange.

Repeat after me:

I got me.

I know.

I am safe with me.

I trust myself.

———

There's a clip of RuPaul talking about being nervous before going on stage. He says:

> "Something I do when I go on stage is pretend I am going on stage in my mother's living room. She loved everything I did. So I act as if the stage is my mama's living room...and that's all Mama out there in the audience. I'm not all nervous and in my head wondering, 'What are they thinking?' I'll tell you what they're thinking...they're thinking, 'Mama loves you. Mama *loves* you! You can do no wrong.' So what you do is imagine you're surrounded by unconditional love. *Unconditional.* And you are able to rise and be the star that you are."

I feel it as I watch the video.

I create the feeling.

I imagine going on stage in RuPaul's living room, and I imagine him loving everything I do.

———

There's a Facebook video that shows a father sitting with his toddler daughter.

She is having an all-out tantrum.

She is by turns sobbing and thrashing and hitting and kicking.

He stays calm and patient, but doesn't let her hit him or hurt herself.

When she comes in for comforting, he holds her and rocks her.

The caption on the video says:

> "That's not a normal fit for her. You could see it had been kind of building for about two weeks, and she just hadn't had the right moment, either she wasn't ready to go for it or we just weren't available to hold space for it. I'm not that patient all of the time, but when I saw that she was going to need me to be, I switched into that mode."

I watch it and cry.

Because it really is that simple.

Unshaming isn't doing.

It isn't fixing. Or improving. Or curing. Or overcoming.

It doesn't require you to massively restructure your life.

Unshaming is a belief and feeling practice.

It is having patience for yourself and for your feelings. All of them.

It's not dismissing or disconnecting from yourself in those moments.

It's reestablishing connection with yourself.

It is meeting yourself as you are, where you are.

Unshaming restores self-respect, connectedness, belonging, authenticity, and radical self-acceptance.

Where shame takes you out of your body, unshaming brings you back home.

————

Put a photo of your younger self in a place where you will see it often.

Look at her and promise not to break her heart.

————

Pay attention to what moves you. Collect those moments. Use them to support you.

CHAPTER 16

LOVE YOURSELF "BECAUSE"

In the Concessions chapter of *Untamed*, Glennon Doyle writes about watching a TV show in which a teenage girl is about to tell her parents that she's gay. The girl says, "I have to tell you something. I like girls." And the mother replies, "We love you no matter what."

Glennon writes that she knows the program is trying to be progressive, to prove that the parents embrace their daughter's gayness just as much as they embrace her straightness.

"I wondered, though," writes Glennon, "if this girl had told her parents that she liked boys, would the mother have said, 'We love you no matter what?' Of course not, because 'no matter what' is what we say when we're disappointed in someone."

> **"'No matter what' is what we say when we're disappointed in someone."**
>
> **—Glennon Doyle**

——

When you've internalized shame, that's how you tend to talk to yourself—as if you're disappointed in yourself. You might not see it that way because you've also internalized the idea that being disappointed in yourself is how you make yourself "better."

You become so used to thinking about yourself with chronic "low-level" shame, self-loathing, and disappointment in yourself (and sometimes even with contempt and disgust) that you can't even see it for what it is. It becomes the air you breathe.

You most likely were not taught to love yourself unconditionally, nor to love others that way.

It might not even be conceivable to you that loving yourself unconditionally is even a thing...that it is possible or even preferable.

And if you were taught to love yourself at all, it was probably only acceptable under very specific conditions:

When you're performing, pretty, pleasing, and polite.

> **"'Unbecoming' is a term that has been used to manipulate and condition girls and women for generations. It's part of the grooming process into the patriarchal trance of unworthiness that keeps us from revealing our true thoughts, feelings, and full self-expression. Like an IV drip inserted at birth, micro-dosing cultural messages such as these have kept us in the 4 Ps: performing, pretty, pleasing, and polite. The 4 Ps condition us to abandon the truth within ourselves in exchange for love and belonging out there. As a result, many of us lose touch with who we truly are underneath all of the layers of the false self."**
>
> **—Monica Rodgers, host of the** *Revelation Project* **podcast**

Getting back to what Glennon wrote, I wondered: What would it look like if I loved myself because of the things I think I should be ashamed of—not in spite of, not even though, not no matter what, but *because of* those things?

I love myself *because* I'm envious and want things I don't have.

I love myself because I am a spoiled brat.

I love myself because I blame others.

I love myself because I want to be seen as a good white woman.

I love myself because I ate a whole bag of potato chips the other day.

I love myself because I was grouchy at the gym.

I love myself because I worry about whether people like me.

I love myself because I was annoyed at my husband because of the way he was breathing.

I love myself because I am so good at sabotaging myself.

I love myself because I am selfish and don't take the time to appreciate others as much as I could.

I love myself because I had a temper tantrum about my work.

I love myself because I am needy and desperate.

I love myself because I was prickly and mean in my head.

I love myself because I'm a people pleaser.

I love myself because I am a show off.

I love myself because I like to be the center of attention.

I love myself because I am disorganized.

I love myself because I worry about reviews of my books on Amazon.

I love myself because I am petty.

I love myself because I am a hypocrite.

That's just one day's list.

It's not a confessional. It's what I came up with having scanned my thoughts about myself over a twenty-four-hour period...the things I say to myself, about myself, and am usually disappointed in myself for.

I know what it's like to feel love in my body, and I really enjoy it. I can feel it as I write this: a warm, welling, expansiveness in my chest that is rising into my throat and making my eyes prickle and shine with tears.

So now, when I think about being a spoiled brat, instead of feeling chronic guilt, shame, self-loathing, and disappointment in myself, I can instead choose to feel that warm, welling, expansiveness in my chest that rises into my throat and makes my eyes prickle with shiny tears.

When I remember to.

So can you.

> "Healing is not becoming the best version of yourself. Healing is letting the worst version of yourself be loved. So many of us have turned healing into becoming this super perfect version of ourselves. That is bondage. That is anxiety waiting to happen. Healing is saying every single version of me deserves love, tenderness, grace. When we get to a place where we can see and empathize with every version of ourselves, even the version of ourselves that we can sometimes be ashamed of...that's when we know we're walking on the path of healing."
>
> —Kobe Campbell, LCMHS, trauma therapist

CHAPTER 17

ON THAT DAY WHEN IT ALL FEELS IMPOSSIBLE, HERE IS YOUR ASSIGNMENT

But how do I love myself and meet myself with compassion?

It's already done. You wouldn't be asking this if you didn't already love yourself.

But I still feel shaky and unsure. I still feel shame.

Do you want to be mean to yourself because you feel shaky and unsure and ashamed?

No.

There's the magic—the love: It's not about never feeling bad or uncomfortable or shaky or unsure or ashamed.

It's about catching yourself before you're mean to yourself.

And in the moments, or hours...or on the days when you feel that way, your only assignment is to...

> **"...love the self that doesn't love herself...until you can love yourself again."**
>
> **—Sonia Renee Taylor, author of** *The Body Is Not An Apology*

PART IV

A TIMELINE OF CONNECTION & RECOVERY

0–5

I Am Born.

My mother counts my fingers and toes.

She says there was a rainbow that day.

Unusual for a Saturday in early November.

Lemon Candy

I am looking at a book in the sewing room in the apartment above the real estate office and beauty parlor.

It's cozy and warm.

My mother gives me a yellow candy shaped like a lemon slice.

She sews.

After school I watch *Captain Kangaroo* and *Lost in Space*.

5–10

Say What I Say

I am visiting my father.

On the car ride we play silly games and laugh.

My favorite game is "Say What I Say." He imitates me as I am talking.

We go to Old McDonald's Farm and see the llamas and ride the ponies.

We go to the ride-through carwash.

My new stepmother reads me *Winnie-the-Pooh*. She does all the different voices.

I Fly by Myself

We drive to Missouri to visit my stepfather's parents.

My mother and stepfather leave me there because my mother has to have surgery.

I fly home on TWA all by myself, and the stewardesses are really nice to me.

10–15

She Grabs Him by the Collar

I'm sitting on the school bus in the very last seat.

The girl next to me pulls the hair of the boy in front of us.

He turns around and punches me in the face.

I tell my mother when I get home.

The next day she goes to the school, finds that boy, grabs him by the collar, and tells him in no uncertain terms that he is never to lay his hands on her daughter again.

Bathing Suit

My stepfather's whole family comes from Missouri for a visit:

His parents and his brother and sister, and their families.

We all pile into a huge camper and drive to Cape Cod.

We stay at a hotel with a built-in pool.

I am embarrassed to be in my two-piece bathing suit.

Aunt Linda tells me how sexy she thinks it is to have a "little bit of a tummy" and not a completely flat one like hers.

I Leap and Dance

I slip outside in the middle of the summer night.

I am wearing a white camisole and long white slip.

I run and leap and dance around the yard.

I lie in the grass and look at the stars.

No one knows.

21+

Hocka Women

I am a junior in college.

My friend Gabe and I get jobs at the farm of Daniel and Jill Pinkwater. The Pinkwaters are children's book authors and artists. They have all kind of animals, and they need the kind of help college students can provide.

And college students (like me) need to be around people like the Pinkwaters.

We called ourself the Hocka Women as we do chores like feeding goats, planting trees, digging ditches, and cleaning out storage cabinets.

And then we have long lunches with Daniel and Jill and we talk about everything.

AOL's Romance Connection

November.

I get my first home computer. It comes with something called America Online.

I am vaguely aware of the Internet.

My best friend comes over and we decide to "sign on." We poke around and find The Romance Connection. There are "chat rooms" and "message boards" for "online" personal ads.

I decide to post an ad for a New Year's Eve date.

Over the course of a couple of months I get more than 250 responses. I respond to about fifty of them. Of those, I speak with about twenty-five on the phone. And of those, I meet ten in person.

Of the ten, there are some that I like, but they're not into me, and there were some who like me a whole bunch, but for me it's a "thanks, but no thanks."

Then there's a response unlike all the rest.

I write back immediately, and before I know it, we're talking on the phone and planning to meet.

———

I walk up to the historic Griswold Inn in Essex and see a guy sitting right inside the door.

It's him. He stands up, and goes up and up! He's tall. He has very blue eyes.

My immediate reaction is that he's not my type.

But I feel something I'm not used to feeling: breezy confidence.

We have dinner and talk easily.

After dinner we go to the Inn's Taproom. A band is playing. We talk and joke, and he puts his arm around me. It feels nice.

It's time to leave. He leans over and kisses me right on the lips and invites me to his place to play Scrabble.

I decline.

I also worry: "Is he like all the rest? Does he just want sex? Will he still be interested if I say no? Why do I care?"

It surprises me. I am not all that attracted to him.

I have a devil-may-care attitude on the outside, but on the inside, I am vulnerable and wary.

We decide to have a second date. It ends similarly to our first.

It's mid-December, and I need to make a decision about New Year's Eve. Since no one better is coming along, I tell him he "wins" the New Year's Eve date.

A Big Glob of Wasabi

New Year's Eve.

The plan is to go to New York City to watch the ball drop in Times Square.

Instead, because the forecast is for a "wintery mix," we stay local, go out for dinner, and then play Scrabble at my place and watch the ball drop on TV.

I consider that he is ninety miles from home and that the weather is not conducive to a long drive late at night.

I choose to be okay with it if he spends the night.

I am on a big sushi kick so I suggest a Japanese place.

He admits to being an unadventurous diner, but is willing to try it as long as there are cooked foods available.

I cajole him into trying a piece of sushi and put a big glob of wasabi on it.

"It's not hot!" I say, innocently. Who *is* this cocky, confident version of me?

That he doesn't get up and walk out right then and there is saying something. Once he gets used to it, he likes the blast of wasabi heat.

The evening progresses. We play Scrabble, drink wine, watch the ball drop, make out, and go to bed.

I awaken in the middle of the night with unpleasant intestinal distress.

I come back from the bathroom in a cold, icky sweat.

Instead of turning away from me or wanting to leave, he wraps me in his arms and holds me.

I experience something I've never experienced.

He does not tell me he loves me (and won't for many months), but in that moment I feel more loved than I ever have in my entire life.

I Meet His Family

He invites me to go to Pennsylvania with him for Thanksgiving.

A man I am dating, and falling in love with, is actually taking me to meet his family!

I exist!

Paris Kisses

The magazine I founded for the trade association I am working for sends me to Paris for a trade show.

I ask the guy to come with me.

We go to a party at the American Embassy.

There's a rainbow.

We discover what we call "Paris Kisses," when couples, who are just walking along, stop for a moment and kiss.

When we get back, my friends ask if we're engaged.

We are not.

I am still afraid I am not worthy of that.

A Kitchen Table Engagement

The magazine is sending me to Paris again.

The guy is coming with me.

At the last minute, the trip is cancelled.

The guy tells me he was planning to ask me to marry him atop the Eiffel Tower.

We get engaged at his kitchen table instead.

We call our families.

And the next time his father sends a family letter, my name is included in the salutation.

A Wedding in Austria

I travel to Vienna, Austria, for my job as the editor-in-chief of a plastics industry trade magazine.

I have been invited to cover the twenty-fifth anniversary celebration of a company that manufactures a range of auxiliary plastics processing equipment (like robots, blenders, loaders, granulators, and dryers).

The first evening there, I meet a woman who is attending with the man she is dating, who works for an injection molding company in Illinois. Unbeknownst to her, the man she is dating is planning not just to propose to her, but also to marry her in Dürnstein, a small village on the Danube (if she says "yes").

He asks.

She says yes!

And she asks me if I will "stand up with her" and be her witness (coincidently, I am spending my fourth wedding anniversary on this trip, and my husband is back at home in Connecticut).

Of course I say "yes."

On September 8, we drive to Dürnstein and they get married.

The next day, I return home, and two days after that, people fly planes into buildings. The editorial I write for the next issue of the magazine isn't about auxiliary plastics processing equipment, it's about the contrast between September 8 and September 11.

It is one of the first things I write that feels like coming home to myself.

I Can Finally Say Those Words

"I love and accept myself."

I Apologize

I call my sister to apologize.

I experience something new.

Instead of being defensive and ashamed in my apology, I am truly sorry.

I see how unconscious shame and self-loathing got me to the point of lashing out so cruelly at my sister.

I Just Send It

I am freelancing.

I pitch an article idea to a local magazine. They decline, but suggest a different topic.

I research and write the article.

I have the urge to send it first to my mother, my husband, my friends, to get their feedback.

Because I think I need them to tell me it's okay. That I am okay.

Something inside me stops me from doing that.

Instead, I just send it to the editor.

They run it as is.

I Write Every Day

Expressing myself via blogging opens something up in me.

I am hungry for self-expression.

Those who follow my blog are hungry for what I have to say.

Although I have called myself "a writer" since 1984, it isn't until now that I feel like a writer.

I write every day.

Writing is saving my life.

Grief Cracks Me Open

10:00 a.m., December 30.

I call my father to tell him what happened with my mother. I tell him that I have cut her out of my life.

He brings up something I hadn't thought about in a long time: that memory I have of them screaming at each other when I was two.

He tells me what happened to cause their fight.

He tells me things he's never been willing to tell me before, things about her and their marriage.

He was always so polite in this way. He never wanted to disparage her to me. He would choose his words very carefully.

But on this day, he tells me so much and so much makes sense.

Before we hang up, he says he's proud of me.

Midnight.

I wake up in a cold sweat.

I barely make it to the bathroom before I pass out on the bathroom floor.

I come to with a weird buzzing in my body...my husband bent over me shaking my shoulders.

It's like all the noise in the world had stopped, and then someone hits the "play" button and it starts back up again.

I ask my husband to bring me a pillow and blanket because I know I will not be leaving the bathroom any time soon.

He goes back to bed.

I lie on the floor, shaking and freezing.

I hear the phone ring. I hear my husband talking. Something is wrong.

He comes to the bathroom door.

"That was your father's wife. Your father had a massive heart attack, and he's not going to make it."

It doesn't happen immediately, but soon enough I am vomiting into the toilet.

Now I am hot and sweaty. I lie back down on the bathroom floor.

How ironic is this?

My father and I share this intense anxiety around throwing up and others throwing up. As debilitating as this anxiety is, it's also something we joke about.

He's dying and I'm puking.

"Thanks, Dad," I say quietly, to no one.

I start to feel a bit better.

I ask my husband to bring me the phone.

I call the number my husband was given. My father's wife answers.

"I need to say goodbye," I tell her. "Can you hold the phone up to his ear?"

There I am, sick on the floor in Connecticut, talking to my basically dead father who is in a hospital in Florida.

"You'd never believe this, Dad," I say. "You're dying and I am throwing up."

I tell him how much I will miss him. And I say goodbye.

He's gone for good about twelve hours later. New Year's Eve, 2010.

At first, I think the wrong parent died.

But no, my father and I were complete.

My mother and I are not.

———

Grief cracks me open. Years later I see my father's death as a catalyst for me to process a lifetime of grief.

I begin to thaw.

Slowly.

The Husband-in-My-Dream

I have a dream.

I am in a room that can only be gotten to by going through another room.

In that other room is a gorgeous woman, lying naked on a bed in a provocative pose.

The husband-in-my-dream walks into that room.

He looks briefly at the woman on the bed and continues past her and walks into my room.

I Will Not Be Quiet

After years of estrangement, my mother sends me a letter in the mail asking what I am going to do to "rectify the situation."

We go back and forth a couple of times, and then she tells me all the things I have done wrong...all the things that she is ashamed of me for.

I imagine her, donning her metaphorical sparring gloves, bobbing and weaving, waiting for me to hit back.

Which is what I did for years.

Instead, I tell her I am confused and that I am not sure what she wants.

She tells me she wants to rehash the past ten years, that she'll send me some articles that may enlighten me, that she doesn't want to lose me, and that she wants to know what caused me to cut her out of my life.

This response has a whole different energy to it, but it's familiar to me: First abuse me, then act all lovey-dovey.

I tell her my confusion is due to her:

- saying that she wants me to rectify the situation
- telling me all the things I have done that she doesn't like or is ashamed of

She's ashamed that I blog about my struggles with my weight.

She's ashamed that I wrote an article for a magazine about how to get a proper bra fitting and used photos of myself in a poorly fitting bra and a bra that fits well. Even though you can't see my face.

I ask her, "In order for me to rectify the situation, do you want me to be ashamed too? Do you want me to apologize for being who I am? I am not ashamed of myself. I am proud of myself."

I tell her to check out Brené Brown.

I tell her vulnerability is not shameful, it is the antidote to shame.

I tell her shame separates and isolates.

I tell her vulnerability connects and that if there's anything that this world needs more of, it's connection and compassion.

What I still haven't realized is that she's not into kindness and compassion.

I tell her that I am *not* responsible for her feelings.

I tell her that she if she wants to feel ashamed of me, then she gets to feel shame.

I tell her that she could also choose to be proud of me, and then she'd get to feel pride.

I tell her that she can choose to love me, and then she'd get to feel love.

I tell her that I am not sure if rehashing the past ten years will get us to where we want to be, but that I can't speak for her.

I ask her what she wants our relationship to look like and how she wants to feel.

I tell her I have nothing left to lose at this point.

She goes silent.

But I...I will *not* be quiet. I refuse to be quiet.

A Tiny Pot of Pink Vaseline Lip Balm

My husband's ex-wife, the mother of his children, is dying.

I go to see her in the hospital on what turns out to be her last lucid day.

I sit next to the bed and tentatively reach for her hand.

"None of this handshake shit," she says. "I want a hug."

After hugging her I sit in awkward silence.

"Hey Mom, how about a milkshake?" her daughter asks.

"I'll get it," I say, jumping up.

I barely make it out of the room before I feel my throat tighten and the sharp prickle of tears behind my eyes.

On the elevator I sob.

"It's so crazy," I say to the two nurses riding down to the cafeteria with me. "My husband's ex-wife is dying. I shouldn't be so upset."

"Oh honey," one of them says as she pats my arm. "You never know how death will affect you."

I return with the milkshake, which remains untouched.

Is she asleep?

"My lips are chapped," she says with her eyes closed.

Her daughter offers Chapstick, which she waves away.

"I want something softer."

There's a tiny pot of pink Vaseline lip balm by the bed.

"Do you want me to put some of this on?" Her daughter asks, holding it up.

"No," she says.

Her son, who is also there, says, "Do you want me to do it?"

Again, no.

I am the only other person in the room.

They look at me, eyebrows raised, and her son asks, "You want Karen to do it?"

She lifts her finger into the air and replies, "Ding ding ding!"

I stick my finger into that tiny pot of pink Vaseline lip balm and carefully dab it on her lips.

Hundreds of Letters

I sit cross-legged on the faded orange carpet in front of the chest of drawers that sits in the tiny office in my grandmother's tiny house.

I am here to clean it out and get it ready for sale.

The air is stale and still.

I open the bottom drawer and find them.

Letters.

Hundreds of letters to and from my grandmother.

I am most interested in the ones to and from my mother.

They start in 1958, the year my mother went away to college.

This is how I begin to learn that it didn't start with me.

College Dream, Evolution 1.5

I have another college dream, but this time, instead of being twenty-one, I am my current age.

I go to an office to get my diploma. Inside it looks like an old-time courtroom.

My mother, stepfather, and husband are there sitting on a long wooden bench.

I stand at the counter and speak to a woman sitting behind a thick glass wall.

I tell her my name, and she goes through her list but can't seem to find me.

Dread wells up briefly, and then I remember.

"Oh, it's probably under my old last name. I got married."

"Hold on, I need to add that to the record," she replies.

She shuffles her papers some more and then hands me (through a slot at the bottom of the glass), a gorgeous, thick, tooled-leather-covered diploma.

It's more like a book. Inside are page after page of all my accomplishments. Some things are seemingly insignificant, but I feel immense pride.

I Take Myself onto My Own Lap

I am crouched down in a squat, on my tippy-toes with my heels touching.

My head is bowed, my chin to my chest, my upper body resting on my thighs, and my fingertips are lightly touching my mat.

My beloved friend and yoga teacher says: "Curl yourself up like a seed and take yourself onto your own lap."

I experience a lovely melting sensation in my chest.

My eyes feel the sharpness of tears-about-to-be-shed.

———

I am sitting in my easy chair, talking with a trusted mentor about something that is hard for me to talk about. I feel myself wanting to shut down.

"Ask your body what it needs," she says.

I lean forward and take myself onto my own lap.

I experience a lovely melting sensation in my chest.

My eyes feel the sharpness of tears-about-to-be-shed.

An Uneasy Truce

Two weeks after her ninety-eighth birthday, my grandmother dies.

I call my mother to let her know.

She and her mother haven't been in contact for many years at this point.

She declines to be present for the small family memorial gathering we have.

Rather than judging her, I understand.

We enter into an uneasy truce.

I Am Still Here

I'm driving down the highway on my birthday, two days after
the election.

My phone buzzes.

It's my mother.

It's been years since she called me on my birthday.

I feel my heart accelerate. I take a deep breath and exhale
long and slow.

I answer the phone through my car's stereo system.

"Happy birthday," she says.

"Thank you."

"How old are you again? It's got to be an even number because you
were born in '62," she says.

"Fifty-four," I reply.

There's a pause.

"How are you, Mom?"

She lets out a sigh and says she's been so stressed out she's about
the election.

I feel the telltale signs of wanting to disappear.

"We're such staunch Trump supporters," she says. "It's been a
roller-coaster."

I am silent. Stunned. Although not.

"Hello? *Hello?*" she says sharply. "Are you still there?"

"Yes, I am here."

"What...you voted for Hillary?" she asks sarcastically.

"Yeah, for me it was anyone but him."

I struggle to maintain my voice and my words.

I pause.

"*Hello?* What are you doing! I can't hear you!" she says angrily.

"I'm on my way somewhere," I reply.

"*You're driving?!* You should know better than to drive and talk on your cell phone."

"I gotta go, Mom. I'll talk to you later."

"But I Wanted You"

My mother comes for a visit for the first time in ten years.

We are sitting on the couch.

"So what do you do all day...sit around and listen to music?" she asks.

"No, I usually spend the morning writing, then I go to the gym, and I see clients in the afternoon. But I've cleared my schedule for your visit."

"Oh, so you're still writing."

"Every day," I reply.

She changes the subject.

"Why didn't you want to have children?" she asks.

Before I can answer, she answers for me, her tone shifting into what I perceive as contempt, "Because you didn't want to have to clean up poopy diapers or hold someone's head while they threw up."

"While that is true, there was no specific reason. I just didn't have the desire. My biological clock never started ticking, I guess."

"Yeah, even as a little girl, you were pretty clear about it," she says, which is news to me. I don't remember it being something from my childhood.

"Based on everything I know about Grandma, everything you've told me about her along with what other people have said and my experience of her, I get the impression that she would've been happier without children," I mention to my mother.

———

I think back to the time when my grandmother was in the nursing home about a year before she died. She lamented to me that she didn't know how to be a good mother to my mother.

"She was defiant and headstrong, just like her father," my grandmother said from her nursing home bed. "I made some mistakes with her."

———

I continue to respond to my mother's question.

"I think I'm like her. Maybe it runs in the family."

To say that I was like her mother, like my grandmother, with some measure of pride, rather than embarrassment or shame, is freeing, because there are very few times I remember my mother speaking about her mother without disdain or contempt.

"She wanted to be like her Aunt Lydia," my mother says. "Her Aunt Lydia was beautiful and married a rich man from Cuba. They lived a glamorous life..."

Her tone of voice shifts in the way it does whenever she speaks of my grandmother.

"Or like her cousin, Yvonne Adair, the Broadway actress."

Neither Aunt Lydia nor Cousin Yvonne had children.

"But Grandpa was a 'family man,'" she says, making air quotes with her fingers.

"I remember him saying that. Of course, he went off to work every day and Mom was stuck with us. She sent me away when I was very little. She didn't want me to have friends or go to kindergarten because she was afraid I'd pick up bad habits, but neither did she want to take care of me. She neglected me."

I remember the three-page, typed, single-space letter I found when I cleaned out my grandmother's home in 2014, a letter my mother had written to her in 1987. It was full of hurt, accusations, and confusion. And in the margins were my grandmother's handwritten notes in response to each accusation: "true," "false," and "This is nuts."

I return to the present moment, look at my mother, and together we say in unison:

"Back then women didn't have much of a choice."

My mother gets a faraway look in her eyes and remembers out loud about having to quit college (reciting the oft-quoted reason her father gave, "because I majored in bridge and boys and flunked out"), marrying my father when she was nineteen even though she was in love with Johnny McIntyre, whom she'd met in college, and how Grandpa kept pestering him to make him a grandfather.

Because he was a family man.

Her voice trails off.

"But I wanted you!" she says, seeming to catch herself.

She has said this before, but this time I hear an unspoken subtext.

I hear, "because I don't think my mother really wanted me, I will make sure you know that I wanted you, even though it would've been nice to finish college and maybe wait to meet and marry a man I really loved."

I respond, "You know, Mom, I would totally get it if you wished you hadn't had a baby under the circumstances in which you had me."

Later I think about the one and only child I was briefly pregnant with. I don't know anything about what that child would have looked like or what kind of personality it would have had.

I didn't reject a specific person. I simply chose not to have a child.

Simply Acknowledge How Painful It Is

I am reading a novel in which one character says to another, "There's no need to feel embarrassed."

The first character wants the second character to feel better. She doesn't want her to feel embarrassed.

Why?

Why do we even say things like this?

You're overreacting.

Don't be so sensitive.

Calm down.

There's no need to feel that way.

Other people's uncomfortable emotions and experiences are uncomfortable for us, and we don't want to be uncomfortable.

And sometimes they're downright inconvenient.

The grief I experience as a two-year-old when my parents get divorced is inconvenient. Stuff has to get done. People have jobs to go to and money to make and things to take care of.

No one (back then) imagines a two-year-old having any awareness of what's happening.

And yet now I know just how intelligent my two-year-old self is when she disconnects herself from that grief so she can survive.

No one has the time or empathy to be cracked open by the messiness of my vulnerability and grief.

It's the same with shame.

I don't want someone to tell me that I shouldn't have this experience.

I want someone to simply acknowledge how painful it is.

I mean, sure, it's hard to watch someone feeling so horribly about themselves.

If I have the courage to name it and acknowledge it, you can name it and acknowledge it too.

Doing so isn't saying that I "should" feel shame...or that I deserve to feel shame, it's simply acknowledging that I experience it.

I Can Because I Already Have

I notice a lone sunflower growing in the empty lot next to ours, and it leads to a profound realization.

Because I am also feeling ever-so-prickly. I am sure it had to do with the last gasps of my menstrual cycle, but what is emerging is that it's really the result of me denying an essential part of who I am, something I've been doing for decades.

Two things bring it to the surface:

1. **I decide, at the last minute, not to attend a writing retreat with the five other women in my writing group.**

2. **I find myself saying "yes" to doing a book signing event that my body was saying "no" to. I eventually decline, but not without a fair bit of internal drama.**

Re #1: In the week leading up to the retreat, I could feel the anxiety ratcheting up in my body. Was it because I had come to fear flying? Yes, but it was more than that. I adored those women. I loved what we had created together. I craved it. So why was I panic-stricken every single time I attended one of our retreats? Once I decided not to go, relief flooded my body. Then came the regret. I knew it would come. Because I want to want this. But I don't.

Re #2: I'm an author. I am supposed to want to do book signings. This was a gracious offer, one that came from someone who is always positive and open to life and wants to help others. But I didn't want to. Just do it. No. What's the big deal? The other authors who did signings there had splashy promotional materials, and my experience tells me that if I invest in splashy promotional materials, I will never use them again. In this case, once I had said "no," it was pure relief, with no regret.

———

I hear my mother's voice:

"If people knew what I was really thinking and feeling, no one would like me."

And, "My mother didn't teach me how be friends with other women."

Me too, Mom. Me too.

I see the results of that thinking on her life. And on my life.

"There's something wrong with me." Shame.

I see how she has isolated herself, cutting herself off from her entire family. And from friends. I hear it in her voice when she tells me that she can't stand the women in her bridge group.

"Those silly women who only care about cookies and desserts. They gossip and giggle. They don't take the game seriously. I prefer to play with men," she spits, echoing my grandmother, who, upon considering a move to an assisted-living facility, retorted: "I couldn't stand to be around a bunch of stupid, talkative women."

Sometimes it's what our mothers say to us, about us, that hurts, but sometimes, it's what our mothers believe about themselves and other women that cuts into us.

In my resistance to not being like my mother, and in her resistance to not being like her mother, we made ourselves wrong for our preferences.

We turned our beautiful, strong, lone-sunflower-selves into combative, defensive, anxious, disgusted selves.

We must not be ourselves because no one will love us. So we do things we don't really want to do and, before we know it, the poison seeps out and either infects those around us or drives them away. We end up alone and miserable, and we die that way.

But why?

Because we were taught to be "nice" rather than learning how to truly occupy ourselves with honesty and kindness.

So we entertain suggestions to do things we do not want to do...rather than being forthright, honest, and kind.

We try to force the lone sunflower shapes of ourselves into something we think will be more pleasing...rather than being forthright, honest, and kind.

Because shame denies us access to forthrightness, honesty, and kindness.

Then we find ourselves riddled with anxiety.

Then we find ourselves wanting to spit with disgust.

Then we recoil with recognition...am I just like her?

Or can we stand forthrightly **and** be honest and kind?

Like this sunflower, that chose to stand alone in the somewhat wild expanse, not in a field of its peers:

I **can** stand forthrightly **and** be honest and kind. I **can** be myself **and** be infinite love.

And be infinitely loved. I can because I already have.

Even Children I Love

It's Christmas Day.

My stepdaughter and her children are about to arrive from Georgia.

Her husband is deployed so they are coming without him.

I am so glad they will be staying at a hotel, even though that's not what my stepdaughter wanted or what my husband wanted when we planned their visit.

I bounce between telling myself I am a selfish, spoiled brat...and telling myself my preferences matter.

I bounce between telling myself my anxiety over having a potentially vomiting child in my house is ridiculous...and telling myself that it's okay for me to take care of myself in this way.

Even though I know I won't die if someone doesn't like me or my choice, my body hasn't caught up.

It occurs to me that maybe, just maybe, my anxiety isn't about other people throwing up, it's the result of me shaming myself for wanting what I want, and not wanting what I don't want.

For not telling the truth, which is that I don't want to be responsible for other people's children. Even children I love.

That I don't want people, even people I love, in my house overnight.

This is a consequence of people-pleasing and of not wanting to "be like my grandmother."

So I pretended.

I agreed to stuff I don't really want to do.

That's on me.

———

During this visit, I am triggered AF.

I am angry and shaming myself for it.

I start to act immaturely.

The whole family, including my two stepsons and their wives, go on a family outing. I don't want to go, but I go anyway.

I act like a petulant teenager (a.k.a. selfish, spoiled brat).

> **hindsight reflection: I am also smack dab in the middle of the hormonal stew of perimenopause**

———

Later, the grandkids and I are having a goofy, silly moment after dinner.

In that way, I am like my dad. I do goofy and silly really well. I **like** goofy and silly. But deep inside, internalized shame is reminding me that it's not okay to be like my dad.

My stepdaughter abruptly announces they're going back to their hotel.

She thinks I am annoyed at the kids.

My husband gets them packed into the car.

When he comes back in, he is angry because he thinks I was being too boisterous with the kids when what they needed was to calm down before bed, and that's why his daughter left with them.

I can't f*cking win.

Everyone is angry at me.

No one understands.

———

The next day, my stepdaughter "scolds" me in front my husband and her kids (who are racing around the room screaming at the tops of their lungs).

She just wants an opportunity to have a break from her children.

I tell her there's a reason I chose not to have children.

She says I need to think of other people.

I feel myself starting to disappear.

But I don't. I stay with myself.

The problem is that I haven't been honest with her about who I am.

Because I haven't been able to be honest with myself about who I am.

Because I have been ashamed of who I am.

And that shame is falling away.

I don't have to shame myself in order to be loved. Contrary to what I experience with my mother.

In this chaotic moment I find a peaceful, untriggered place inside myself and I take responsibility for not being honest about who I am.

The word "dignity" floats up.

I will be treated with dignity and that must start with me.

I think about what I have done for my stepdaughter, happily and without resentment, because I wanted to. And how I will continue to. But I will not lie to her any more about who I am.

We will find our way.

I Could So Easily Slip into Shame

That essay I read on the Listen To Your Mother stage about my relationship with my step kids' mother?

It gets published on the *O Magazine* website.

It happens quickly. I email my step kids to let them know it's going live the next day.

There's a part of me that knows I am not handling it the way I want to. I push that aside.

A few weeks go by.

My stepdaughter calls because she is upset that...

1. **I didn't give her much notice about the piece being published**

2. **There were things I shared in the essay that weren't mine to share**

Her voice is shaking. She is close to tears.

I agree with her.

I apologize.

It's not fun or easy to have this conversation.

I could so easily slip into shame, but I don't.

I could so easily disappear, but I don't.

I could so easily make this mean I am bad, but I don't.

I am proud of her for speaking up.

I am proud of me for having expanded the capacity of my nervous system, so I am not triggered into a shame freeze.

I tell her that I will email the editor and ask that the part that's not mine to share be deleted.

She asks me if I will let her know if I write about her or her mother in the future. I agree.

She thanks me for that (and she has given me her blessing to the parts of this book that include her).

I Don't Have to Wait for the Good Mood Fairy

> "Someone being patient with you is one of the purest
> forms of love."
>
> —from a photo of a poster on a bus stop shelter on a city
> street somewhere

I am in a foul mood.

I carry it with me, purposefully, like a heavy purse that keeps sliding off
my shoulder as I'm trying to do things.

It pulls at me as I make lunch.

It comes with me on a hike with my husband.

It's with me as I play Words With Friends and do the New York Times
crossword puzzle.

I don't enjoy any of it. I don't want to enjoy anything.

The sensations of it are interesting. A sort of swirling, whirling heaviness
in my chest. A squintiness in my eyes. A taut jaw. I want to snarl
and sneer and roll my eyes (and do so in my head, or when no one
is looking).

I send myself to bed early.

I tell my husband I'm in a bad mood and he says can tell. He asks why,
and my knee-jerk response is a snippy "I don't know," and then a
softer "It's not you."

But I do know.

I am in a bad mood because I am telling myself it's not okay to be
envious about something.

I want something I don't have, and I tell myself I am a spoiled brat.

I ruminate and stew about it all day long.

Rather than just letting myself be envious and loving myself because I am envious, I layer shame and judgment on top.

I let my husband hug me goodnight but tell him that I am temporarily disdainful of hugs.

———

I have learned to let my husband love me when I am in a bad mood, but, on some level, I still don't think I deserve it, not to mention I'm not loving myself.

When I'm in a bad mood, I accept it, but I don't love myself.

And there's a difference. Do I love myself at other times? For sure.

But in this moment, I see once again that my self-love is conditional.

It is not available when shame is talking and labeling me as a selfish, spoiled brat.

I tell myself I'm not fit to be around people.

I punish myself for my desires and my bad moods...for feeling emotions I deem bad and wrong and ugly.

My shame may not have started with me, but I am the one responsible for it now.

And this is good news, because it means I don't have to wait for the Good Mood Fairy to sprinkle magic dust on me in order to love myself again.

I don't have to wait for Mommy to tell me it's okay to come out of my room.

I don't have to force myself into being happy before I am ready so I can be around people again.

Yes, I forgot my promise to myself to love myself "because."

I love myself because I forgot.

I Am Afraid of Hurting People

Because I am still afraid of experiencing shame.

I don't quite trust myself not to shame myself.

Because shame doesn't knock.

And yet I still hurt people. People I love.

And people I don't even know.

One time I hurt someone I don't know (unintentionally) and at the same time got an overwhelming amount of positive feedback.

This person had sent me a message on Facebook telling me that while she respected me for my work around difficult mother-daughter relationships, I needed to "be quiet" about my political beliefs. She told me that my opinions should be kept quiet and that due to my "political outbursts and clear disregard for those who disagree," she and others might unfollow me.

I decide to make a post on Facebook using her words (anonymously) and my response to her as an example of the kind of "protective" shaming that happens not just between mothers and daughters but between women.

Two things happen.

Number One.

There is an overwhelming wave of positive response and acknowledgement.

As my Facebook post explodes with likes and loves, at first, I feel amazing, and then *bam*, I start to disconnect.

Cue a nervous system freeze with a massive side of shame.

Sometimes, when I experience shame for something, it's because I'm giving my brain the wrong instructions about that thing being shameful, or my body perceives a threat that isn't actually there.

In this case, my brain is telling me I am not just bad, but bad to the f*cking bone, for liking the attention I am getting.

I've trained myself to feel shame in these kinds of situations.

> **"Shame is not smoke that indicates there's a fire.
> Shame is smoke that indicates you told your brain to
> produce smoke when you do that thing.
> There's no actual fire. It's a false alarm."**
>
> **—Kara Loewentheil, host of the** *Unf*ck Your Brain* **podcast**

Number Two.

The next day, the woman sends me an email telling me how hurt she was by my sharing her words and that she has emailed the CEO of the company that publishes my books, letting him know what I've done.

In that slightly frozen and destabilized place, I am unable to honor boundaries that are part of my self-care.

I travel even further from my center.

I defend and explain something I don't want to defend or explain.

I people please, trying to impress someone whom I want to like me, by saying something on a Facebook post that I don't actually believe, and in so doing, I offend a client, whom I didn't even know was friends with the person I am trying to impress.

I am disappearing from myself.

Then, in one of those "the universe has my back" moments, I decide to catch up on *This Is Us* and see the episode where Randall goes to New Orleans and learns about his birth mother's life.

He screams in a lake.

And I cry.

Deep, heaving, cleansing, and snotty.

And I rock myself.

And I ask my husband to hug and rock me.

And from that thawed and more stable place, I am able to remember that I no longer need to be afraid of hurting people in order not to hurt them.

Crying is intelligent. It is stabilizing. It is regulating.

"You shall be saved in an ocean of tears."

—Gordon Neufeld, child development expert and psychologist

I Growl

We're visiting my mother and her husband.

We order takeout.

Unbeknownst to me, the meal I order has kidney beans in it.

I hate kidney beans. They're like lima beans.

I pick the beans out and put them aside.

"Why don't you like beans?" my mother says with a tone I know to mean, "I know you hate beans, but I am going to tease you about it."

Anger rises. A boundary has been crossed. I trust my experience.

I am no longer a powerless child being made to eat lima beans.

"I don't like the taste or texture."

She rolls her eyes and says, "But beans have so much protein and fiber in them."

I squint my eyes just a little bit, clench my jaw just a little bit, bare my teeth just a little bit, and *ever so slightly* lean toward her.

I literally growl and disguise it as clearing my throat.

"It's a good thing other foods have protein and fiber in them," I say.

She backs off.

It Was Never Mine

"Do you think your mother or grandmother ever felt like a pathetic loser?" a trusted mentor asks me.

"No, I can't imagine that," I reply. "There's no way my mother has ever felt like a pathetic loser."

But I let my mind wander. I think about the things I know my mother and grandmother went through, and I realize it's likely both of them had shame-based experiences that resulted in them having pathetic loser-like thoughts about themselves, even if they didn't use those specific words.

Then the truth rushes through me:

"It didn't start with me!" I exclaim. "It's not mine. It's not *mine! It's not mine!*"

I pound my desk for emphasis.

And, I realize, it's not theirs either.

Later, much later, I lie in bed and my stomach hurts.

I need to vomit.

My body is deciding to make sure I really and truly get it.

A vision comes to me as I lie there.

A long line of women standing next to each other, stretching into infinity.

The first woman has handed a box to the second woman, who takes it with one hand and, without examining its contents, tucks it inside, and then uses her other hand to take it out and hand it to the next woman, who does the same with the third woman, and so on down the line.

Each time the box changes hands, it looks a little different, but inside... inside is the same message: I'm not okay. I'm unworthy. There is something wrong with me. I am bad.

It was handed to me in a package that looks different than the one it was originally received in. That's why it feels so personal.

So shameful.

What if I am the last woman in that line?

What if it ends with me?

Can it end with me?

I now know that it is not mine.

That it was never mine.

It was handed to me in a package that looks like it was meant for me.

But it's not.

But Nah

My husband gets bitten by a dog at the dog park and needs stitches and a series of rabies shots.

While he is off doing that, I google "side effects of rabies shots" and find that nausea and vomiting are side effects.

I feel the sensations I know to be anxiety: weak knees, shallow breathing, difficulty swallowing, flutters in my chest, eyes squinty and tense.

I don't like it.

I would prefer not to feel it.

But feel it I do.

My brain offers me a bunch of thoughts about the situation and the sensations I am feeling in my body.

And I am able to let myself be present for it.

I don't judge or shame myself for feeling it.

I don't get angry at it or at myself.

I don't make it mean anything.

I don't even try to get rid of it.

I am tempted to think "It's about f*cking time," but even that thought isn't all that sticky anymore.

I am tempted to regret all the times I let anxiety impact my relationships with others.

But nah.

I see it for what it is: an opportunity to be in integrity with myself.

To be true to myself.

To tell myself the truth.

I see all the times it tried to get my attention...and all the times I resisted.

Anxiety is common. It's often called a disorder. It is said to develop from a complex set of risk factors, including genetics, brain chemistry, personality, and life events.

For me, going through perimenopause was a significant factor, and while I am sure there are hormonal connections during midlife for most humans who have a uterus and a menstrual cycle, is a time to remember who we are...to tell ourselves the truth...to be in integrity with ourselves...to live unshamed.

I Write Beautiful Things

My stepfather's wife dies from kidney cancer that was discovered less than a month prior.

Jane and I had a close relationship spanning more than thirty years.

When I find out she has maybe a week to live and isn't conscious most of the time, I make arrangements to fly to where she is, even though I don't want to.

I watch myself struggle with this decision.

I watch my brain warning me, if you don't go what will everyone think? They will be hurt and mad. They will think you're a selfish, spoiled brat. You need to have a really good excuse not to go. You need to have a reasonable explanation.

My husband says, "Whether you go or not, one thing I know for sure is that you will write something beautiful about Jane."

My body floods with sensations that I know to be love and truth.
He is right.

I cancel the travel arrangements.

I don't explain, other than to say I am not coming.

And then I write something beautiful about Jane.

"I write beautiful things" becomes a thought that takes up more space in my brain than "I'm a selfish, spoiled brat."

I Let My Face Light Up

I am getting ready to do an outdoor thing with my husband and his oldest son and his son's wife.

It's hot and humid.

My body has changed.

I don't know what to wear.

So when my husband says breezily, "Put on cooler clothes," I want to scream and snarl at him. I want to say, "How many f* cking times do I have to tell you I hate this f* cking weather?"

I don't do that.

This isn't new. I've felt this way every summer, no matter what size and weight and shape my body is.

And on this hot and humid day I find myself in that place again.

I pray the forecasted thunderstorms will make us cancel it.

I feel mean. I change my clothes over and over again, getting sweatier and more furious in the process.

I finally give in and wear the thing that is cool, but to my angry mind, unflattering.

I am squinty eyed and disgusted with myself as I look at my reflection in the mirror.

Something shifts.

I look at myself again and the disgust...melts.

Because it's not mine.

I was not looking at myself through my eyes.

I let my face light up.

And the urge to scream and snarl and offload my disgust and fury dissipates.

College Dream, Evolution 2.0

It turns out that, yup, it's true, I haven't actually done the work, and I hadn't met certain requirements, nor have I honored commitments like practicing my part in a play or showing up to the performance.

I don't even tell anyone I'm not doing it. They all show up on stage and I...don't.

There's no dread or shame. I just tell them that I am tired and am changing my mind.

"You can keep the diploma. I'm good."

The Truth Will Never Make Us Suffer

My grandmother is on my mind lately.

I thought about her a couple of weeks ago when I spoke with a group of women who are caring, in one way or another, for their elderly mothers, some of whom have memory issues.

I thought about her again when an online conversation turned to the subject of pleasure and masturbation as a way for women to create and be open to success, abundance, and sufficiency.

What would my senile grandmother have to do with a conversation about masturbating?

Well, the day before she died, she masturbated. She was ninety-eight. Ninety-eight years old. And I know she did because I was there, in her nursing home room, with her. There was no mistaking it. I didn't know she'd die the next day, but I knew she was close.

And that conversation about self-pleasure and abundance?

When my grandmother was in her sixties, she started dating a very wealthy man. They never married, but when he died, he left pretty much everything to her. Did she understand, on some level, that her pleasure was connected to her abundance? Maybe. And she also lived through the Depression and was considered a frugal person by most everyone who knew her.

Here's what I believe my grandmother wanted for herself:

If she could have lived the life she wanted, she would have been a model or an actress. She wouldn't have gotten married and she wouldn't have had children, at least not when she did. She would have had as many men as she wanted, and she would have lived alone.

What she actually did is marry my grandfather when she was twenty-one, in 1939, and then had three children, while also having multiple affairs. They eventually divorced in 1980. She was sixty-two.

My grandmother was a pleasure-seeker at a time and in a world that doesn't approve of that for women (and pretty much still doesn't).

But it didn't stop her. When I was getting her house ready for sale, I found sexy photos of her over the years. From her twenties up through her seventies and maybe even eighties.

There was my elderly grandmother, nude in a bathtub, with a come-hither look on her face.

(Of course, this is my perception of a life I didn't know all that much about...I can't know all the ins and outs of my grandmother's thoughts and feelings.)

I shared this with the women I was chatting with, adding, "This may all sound so glamorous and badass, but she was also living with a lot of shame. My mother was hurt and disgusted by her mother's behavior and grew to hate her because my grandmother preached being a 'good girl' to her."

It was very much a "Do as I say, not as I do" deal.

By the time I became her guardian, I knew her as a complicated woman who was, by turns, anxious, bitter, and mean. Sometimes funny. Warm and loving, rarely. I saw her through my mother's filter, through all the judgment of my grandmother as a hypocritical homewrecker and gold digger.

In the end, she got what she wanted...she was well-resourced, lived by herself, and wasn't financially dependent on anyone.

And then there's the way it played out in my mother's life, marrying my father at nineteen after she "flunked out of college," having me at twenty-two because her father wanted her to make him a grandfather, and then a couple of years later, getting on a plane, by herself, in 1965, so she could fly to Mexico and get a "quickie" divorce because it wasn't legal for a woman to get divorced in Connecticut then.

And the way it played out in mine, marrying a guy from Brazil who needed a green card, because I didn't think I was good enough for a man to actually love me.

Whereas my grandmother and mother were model-thin and beautiful, I was chunky and awkward. And beautiful.

The shame was so pervasive we couldn't see it...it's the water we have been swimming in for...ever.

And it wasn't ours.

It's what makes us hypocrites. It's what makes us narcissists. It's what makes us rigid and needy and manipulative. It's what makes us emotionally neglectful with our children. It's what makes us abusive (or turn a blind eye to abuse). It's what makes us hate our mothers. It's what makes us jealous of our daughters. It's what drives us mad. It's what makes us hate our bodies. It's what makes us contract with desperation. It's what turns us off. It's what keeps us small. It's what silences us. Makes us bitter. Depressed. Anxious. Traumatized. Living in what feels like a forever pattern of fight, flight, freeze, or fawn.

So many of us...and so many of our mothers...so many amazing, badass women...are drowning in shame *that is not ours!*

It was never ours. Never.

One way we can step out of it and unshame ourselves is by telling the truth about our lives, knowing that the truth will never make us suffer.

We can tell the stories of our mothers and their mothers through an unshamed lens.

We can learn to find pleasure in ourselves.

Here's to our collective unshaming and to our pleasure, our abundance, our sufficiency, and our success.

Be a cycle-breaker. Be proud. Know and honor your lineage. And have healthy, mature boundaries.

A Friday Afternoon. I'm Grocery Shopping.

"Stop dancing in the aisles!" the woman whisper-shouts, teeth bared, hands clenched, at the two girls with her (her granddaughters?).

The girls shrink.

I lock eyes with an older gentleman as we navigate the crowded produce section.

I smile.

He dances a little jig.

"May you always feel free to dance in the aisles," I say to him, and to the girls, with a wink, who are watching behind their grandmother's back.

He nods and smiles.

Meanwhile, a young man turns to the woman with him and says, "Should I make a cobbler?"

She doesn't reply.

"I think the answer to that question is always 'yes,'" I say in a low voice, with a smile, which he can't see behind my mask, but he can feel it.

"Thanks," he replied, in an equally low voice.

EPILOGUE

Our fifteen-year-old cat, Bella, is declining. She's been struggling with thyroid and other issues for a while and has lost significant weight.

Two weeks before I submit the first draft of this manuscript, we arrange for her to be euthanized.

The day comes, and the grief is intense. It's not that I didn't expect it. But it has been a while since I experienced it so acutely.

There is something else present, although I don't see it at first. Because it didn't knock.

Grief is a cauldron of feelings, a roiling, boiling stew of sorrow, love, regret, guilt, distress, and yes, shame. At least for me, this time.

My very first shame-based thought, "I am bad," still lives within me, my brain has handed it to me, and in this unguarded and vulnerable moment, I take it.

Because I am receiving so much care and love from friends and family who know I am grieving Bella's loss and there's still a part of me (although it's a very small part now) that believes I don't deserve it...

...because in the past year I lost my patience a time or five with Bella and her incessant meow-screaming (especially in the middle of the night) and I screamed back at her.

How human of me.

So, there I was, late in the afternoon of the day Bella died, sobbing, when I realized that my grief was tinged with shame.

So as my husband held me and cried with me, I let it go. Again.

Life will always give me an opportunity to practice.

And that seems like a good place to wrap this up.

Because there will be days when you forget.

You don't realize that you have put the glasses back on.

Does this mean you haven't released it and are not healed
and recovered?

What even is recovery?

According to the dictionary, it is "a return to a normal state of health,
mind, or strength."

"Normal"? Really?

It is also "the action or process of regaining possession or control of
something stolen or lost."

What was stolen was your inherent dignity and worthiness.

So what is recovery from shame?

Abstaining from the idea that there is a "normal." Intentionally.

Remembering when you forget, because you will forget.

Regaining possession of worthiness.

Repossessing it when you lose it, because you will.

Defining what that looks like for you.

And redefining it when necessary, because your perspective
will change.

It is not proving that you've overcome it all and are now perfect.

It is not demonstrating that you have achieved a level of healing determined by someone else.

That's the problem with writing a book like this.

That's the problem with reading a book like this.

There is no "there" there.

There is no "eternal sunshine of the spotless mind."

There is just being a human—a human who may get to the point of asking to be shown the truth about their own inner being.

The wound starts to heal—not when you get rid of it, but when you no longer shame yourself for having it.

BIBLIOGRAPHY

Albina, Victoria. VictoriaAlbina.com.

Bedrick, David. *UnShame Your Life*. davidbedrick.com.

Brown, Brené. brenebrown.com.

Campbell, Kobe. KobeCampbell.com.

DeYoung, Patricia A. *Understanding and Treating Chronic Shame*. Routledge, 2015.

Doyle, Glennon. *Untamed*. Dial Press, 2020.

English, Melanie. melanieenglish.com.

Gilbert, Elizabeth. *Eat, Pray, Love*. Bloomsbury UK, 2010.

Johnson, Kimberly Ann. *Call of the Wild*. HarperCollins, 2021.

Jones, Saeed. *How We Fight for Our Lives*. Simon & Schuster, 2019.

King, Stephen. *Fairy Tale*. Simon and Schuster, 2022.

Libretexts. "Titration—Chemistry LibreTexts." *Chemistry LibreTexts*, Libretexts, 2 Oct. 2013. chem.libretexts.org.

Lyon, Bret. Center for Healing Shame, healingshame.com.

Maddox, Rachael. *ReBloom*. 2021.

Martinez, PsyD, Mario. *The Mind-Body Code*. 2016.

Maté, Gabor. drgabormate.com.

McDonald, MaryCatherine. *Unbroken: The Trauma Response Is Never Wrong*. Sounds True, 2023.

Rein, Valerie. *Patriarchy Stress Disorder: The Invisible Inner Barrier to Women's Happiness and Fulfillment*. Lioncrest Publishing, 2019.

Rum, Etaf. *A Woman Is No Man*. HarperCollins, 2019, p. 280.

RuPaul. rupaul.com.

Somatic Experiencing® International, traumahealing.org.

Stephen W. Porges, PhD | Polyvagal Theory, stephenporges.com.

Taylor, Sonya Renee. *The Body Is Not an Apology*. 2018.

Tippett, Krista. "Richard Davidson—A Neuroscientist on Love and Learning | The On Being Project." *The On Being Project*, www.facebook.com/OnBeing, onbeing.org/programs/richard-davidson-a-neuroscientist-on-love-and-learning-feb2019.

Walker, Pete. *Complex PTSD: From Surviving to Thriving*. Createspace Independent Publishing Platform, 2013.

Wise, Ally. Instagram, www.instagram.com/awakenwithally.

A SURPRISE CHAPTER WHERE YOU WOULDN'T THINK TO FIND ONE

"The revolution will NOT be psychologized.
The revolution will be alchemized.
The revolution will be ancestoralized.
The revolution will be an offering.
The revolution will be a flood of grace.
The revolution will be ritualized.
The revolution will be poeticized."

—From *The Emerald* podcast episode entitled, "The Revolution Will Not Be Psychologized" by Joshua Michael Schrei

When we are born, we have both the fire of the opal and the watery coolness of oceans within us. Like a golden glass orb, we are shiny, complete, and whole.

And just as glass can be broken, we are given the idea that our hearts and spirits could also shatter...and they can. What's true is that our shattered hearts and spirits do not signify inherent flaws or brokenness.

So we live with our hearts and spirits shattered and broken by shame, and we learn to shame ourselves even more with the stories we tell ourselves about ourselves.

One day a long time ago, we internalized a story that wasn't ours and isn't true...that was never true:

I'm bad! I'm pathetic! I'm a loser! I'm worthless. I'm unlovable. I will never get over it, and it will always be a problem. It is written in the stars that I should be ashamed of myself.

For a while, we were unconscious to these stories, clinging to them and never imagining there could be a different one.

What we didn't know is that the story itself was broken.

So for a while we let it hurt us...and then we let it ignite passion and purpose.

This is the gift of unshaming.

Rather than believing that beauty could only exist in perfection and symmetry, we now know, deep inside, that beauty lies in shifting impermanence and imperfection.

We are not shattered and fractured and broken—the story that we are doesn't represent the whole of our lives, but rather moments in our histories.

Now we choose not to hide our so-called flaws from inspection, but rather to emblazon them with golden significance so we can see the full and profound shape of ourselves.

We embrace and accept what we once saw as brokenness, knowing now that it was fierce and strong and intelligent all along.

We know how to be true to ourselves.

Because there are parts of us that never, ever believed that false story.

There are parts of us, parts that existed before we were even born, that know that story isn't true.

No matter what they said.

Because we are unshamed.

This is our birthright and our identity. We might see it outside ourselves, but what we see out there is also within us, not just us alone but together.

Understanding this lays a foundation for engaged dreaming and for guiding desired change.

We know what it is like to dream from the place of "not good enough" and to believe that someone else has the answers.

Now we dream from the place of already knowing and of already having.

We allow ourselves to be pulled toward what we desire rather than pushing away what we don't want.

We already have much that we desire.

We have desires that we have not yet met.

We are shedding that which we do not need or want.

And we are clear about what we don't have and don't want.

We already embody everything that we sometimes believe is out there beyond our reach.

We are creating our identity and making meaning of it over and over again, traveling an upward spiral as we revisit our story from a higher place.

It's the same story through a different lens at a different time, but still our own immanent souls.

We are the hard and the soft, the big F*ck you and the gentle namaste, the muck of self-loathing and the hands-over-heart mudra (gesture) of self-compassion.

We are rich, deep red-purple-gold, spicy chocolate, velvety moss.

We are a giddy sandalwood drumroll!

A slow and steady strut.

Mischievous! Exhilarated! Generous! Content! Grace-full! Vital!

We summon profound self-trust, compassion, equanimity, and
deep listening.

We cultivate autonomy, resilience, eloquence, assertiveness,
and observing.

We stand for justice, self-realization, integrity, and ultimately for
community actualization.

We stand with our hands on our hips, present to the humans of wonder
that we are.

We love deeply. We step forward. There is no veneer.

Our voices hum and shiver and create.

We speak truth, with no swords on our tongues.

We are unshamed.

We are ourselves. Together.

Much, much love,

Karen

(written in partnership with Trish McAvoy Reyburn)

P.S.

___

Thank you for being a part of my world and for letting me be a part of yours.

Stay in touch by signing up for my email Love Notes (answers to your questions, advice, excerpts from books, offers, and other bits of wisdom delivered to your inbox): ww.kclanderson.com/subscribe.

I am most active on Facebook (www.facebook.com/KCLAnderson) and also have a presence on TikTok (www.tiktok.com/@kclanderson) for as long as we are allowed to have TikTok.

If you are interested in having one-on-one guidance on your unshaming journey, please send me an email: karen@kclanderson.com.

Thanks for reading!

ACKNOWLEDGEMENTS

Brenda Knight, thank you for saying no to this book the first time I proposed it to you. Thank you for coming back to me and being open to the idea of *me* writing *this* book. Thank you for your patience and guidance. And to the entire team at Mango, especially Robin Miller, Elina Diaz, and A*, what you were able to make happen in a relatively short amount of time is nothing short of spectacular!

David Bedrick, thank you for being willing to flip the paradigm of shame on its head.

Beth Edelstein, thank you for trying out these concepts over and over again, for telling me when you don't understand, and for sharing your advice and wisdom about the publishing industry.

Christie Inge, thank you, deeply, for your friendship.

Lynn Gaffin, thank you thank you thank you for your gentle guidance and for coming into my life at the moment I most needed you.

My beloved clients, past, current, and future, thank you for your courage, your honesty, and your vulnerability. We are doing this!

Tim Anderson, just writing your name makes me cry with gratitude. Thank you, always, for being a force for unshaming in my life.

ABOUT THE AUTHOR

Karen C.L. Anderson is a human who experiences shame and who helps other people who experience shame to use the power of storytelling to unshame themselves. Her coaching practice is trauma-aware and based on intersectional feminist principles.

She is also the international bestselling author of *Difficult Mothers, Adult Daughters: A Guide for Separation, Liberation & Inspiration*, *The Difficult Mother-Daughter Relationship Journal*, and *Overcoming Creative Anxiety: Journal Prompts & Practices*.

She holds an Advanced Certification in Feminist Coaching, a Master Life Coach Certification from the Life Coach School, is a Dare To Lead Trained Professional, A Healthy Boundaries for Kind People coach and facilitator, and is an Emotional Freedom Techniques practitioner (EFT Training For Trauma, Levels I + II).

She lives in Southeastern Connecticut. Her website is at kclanderson.com.

Mango Publishing, established in 2014, publishes an eclectic list of books by diverse authors—both new and established voices—on topics ranging from business, personal growth, women's empowerment, LGBTQ studies, health, and spirituality to history, popular culture, time management, decluttering, lifestyle, mental wellness, aging, and sustainable living. We were named 2019 *and* 2020's #1 fastest growing independent publisher by *Publishers Weekly*. Our success is driven by our main goal, which is to publish high quality books that will entertain readers as well as make a positive difference in their lives.

Our readers are our most important resource; we value your input, suggestions, and ideas. We'd love to hear from you—after all, we are publishing books for you!

Please stay in touch with us and follow us at:

Facebook: Mango Publishing
Twitter: @MangoPublishing
Instagram: @MangoPublishing
LinkedIn: Mango Publishing
Pinterest: Mango Publishing
Newsletter: mangopublishinggroup.com/newsletter

Join us on Mango's journey to reinvent publishing, one book at a time.

CPSIA information can be obtained
at www.ICGtesting.com
Printed in the USA
JSHW032231010623
42540JS00004B/4